BG347D

BG3476D

Donaldson.

King George VI and Queen

Elizabeth.

1977

KING GEORGE VI
AND QUEEN ELIZABETH

KING GEORGE VI AND QUEEN ELIZABETH

FRANCES DONALDSON

J. B. LIPPINCOTT COMPANY
PHILADELPHIA AND NEW YORK

Copyright © 1977 by Frances Donaldson

Printed in Great Britain

U.S. Library of Congress Cataloging in Publication Data

Donaldson, Frances Lonsdale, Lady.
  King George VI and Queen Elizabeth.

  Includes index.
  1. George VI, King of Great Britain, 1895–1952.
2. Elizabeth, consort of George VI, 1900–
3. Great Britain—Kings and rulers—Biography.
4. Great Britain—Queens—Biography. I. Title.
DA584.D6   941.084′092′2 [B]   77–5122
ISBN-0-397-01229-2

CONTENTS

INTRODUCTION

O F THE LAST SIX British sovereigns, only two, Edward VII and
Edward VIII, were born Heir Apparent. When one looks for the
reasons why the British monarchy should have survived into the present age, adapting itself to the changing times, if not as much as some
people have proposed that it should, at least as much as the majority of the population
desire, this may well be one of them. In the succession of George V there was an
element of pure luck. His elder brother, Prince Albert Victor (Prince Eddy), while
personally charming, was by character and temperament unsuitable to be King. He
had feeble health and he has been described as having 'an inert, apathetic nature',
as being 'backward and utterly listless', and more picturesquely as 'aimless as a
gleaming goldfish in a crystal bowl'. When he died at the age of twenty-seven, he
was much mourned by his family and the nation, but he was clearly not the stuff
through which the monarchy might have been preserved in a period that saw the
disappearance of most of the crowned heads of Europe.

In addition, it may be argued that, quite apart from the accident which in this
case substituted a good and able King for one who must inevitably have been danger-
ously weak, to be born at the centre and apex of a world which compounds so many
of the elements of fantasy, may cast too great a burden on any but the strongest
mind. We have the example of Edward VIII to encourage this belief, and we may
hold with certainty the view that follows from it, that it has been of benefit to the
monarchy that so many of our Kings and Queens have passed their formative years
in circumstances which, if unusual were not unique, and which were comparatively
free from responsibility and homage. 'I will be good', the young Victoria said when
she learned that she was next in succession to the throne, and one can feel the impact
in her words of the tremendous thing that had happened to her. A similar sense
of awe and dedication seems to have been experienced by George V, George VI and
Elizabeth II when they learned in turn that theirs would be the supreme position.
We know that George V, travelling in India as heir to the throne, received 'a notion
which was to grow in strength until it dominated his life, of what must henceforth
be expected of the man or woman called to wear the Imperial Crown'.

It was this great expectation that George VI was so bitterly aware of when the crown was thrust upon him in circumstances of shame and disorder for which he was as little prepared as he was for his accession: and the response to it could be seen on his daughter's face when, for the first time, television showed their sovereign to the British people at the moment of consecration. The monarchy could hardly have survived in modern times without the dedication of generation after generation of this family.

There is still another reason to think it felicitous that George VI was born the second son of his father. George V himself as long ago as 1886, writing to his mother about the marriage of his elder brother Prince Albert Victor, said 'I feel that it would be much nicer if he married an English person ... but I am afraid that both Grandmamma & dear Papa wish him to marry a German.' Germany, so strong in small principalities, was the breeding ground for princesses of the royal blood. By 1923 the Great War had made marriage to an English girl even more attractive and had decimated the royal families of Europe. Nevertheless, when the second son of the King married Lady Elizabeth Bowes-Lyon, it was the first time for more than two hundred years – since James II, as Duke of York, married Lady Anne Hyde – that the son of an English king had married a commoner. It cannot be assumed that at that time the same freedom would have been allowed the Prince of Wales.

Through his marriage to Lady Elizabeth, George VI secured the dynasty of Windsor (the name adopted by George V for the Royal House during the First World War). When the mother of the children of the King was at last a person of British descent there occurred in genetical terms a highly desirable 'out-cross', which brought vigour as well as national characteristics to the old German strains. This might have been foreseen. What was not predictable was that the beneficent fate which had substituted George V for Prince Albert Victor and George VI for Edward VIII should have ordained that the future Queen Elizabeth would bring to her marriage a natural talent for the social arts required of her, combined with a sense of duty which is vocational. For more than fifty years she has dedicated herself to the British people, and the history of George VI's reign will never be written without reference to the part she played at the time of the Abdication, during the Second World War and in the long revolutionary years which followed it.

ONE

PRINCE ALBERT

A LITTLE TO THE DISMAY of his parents, George VI was born on 14 December 1895, the anniversary of the death of the Prince Consort. His family seem to have been genuinely uncertain whether Queen Victoria would look upon the new arrival as a blessing sent to alleviate the sadness of the terrible day, or as a hapless intruder whose maladroit entry into the world would forever prejudice her against him.

Edward VII (who was then Prince of Wales but will be referred to throughout as Edward VII) wrote to his son (then Duke of York) that the Queen had been a little distressed and he said: 'I really think it would gratify her if you yourself proposed the name *Albert* to her.' This advice, combined with the generally apologetic air by which her family showed that they were not insensitive to her feelings, mollified the baby's great-grandmother, who wrote to the Duchess of York: 'I am all impatience to see the *new* one, born on such a sad day but rather the more dear to me, especially as he will be called by that dear name which is a byword for all that is great and good.'

With this regal blessing the child, who would one day be King, was christened at Sandringham church on 17 February 1896, receiving the names Albert Frederick Arthur George. The name 'Albert', which nearly all the Royal Family bore as first or second name, but which is apparently not thought suitable for a king, has the rather charming diminutive 'Bertie', already made famous by his grandfather. By this name the new baby would be known to his family.

Prince Albert was born at York Cottage, one of the strangest of royal residences. It had originally been built for the overflow of guests from the big house at Sandringham. It was given by the Prince of Wales to the Duke of York on the occasion of his marriage to Princess May of Teck. From that time it was consistently extended to hold the increasing family and the numerous attendants of the Duke and Duchess of York. Many biographers have described York Cottage but it is virtually impossible to give a credible account of this incredible house, or of the poverty of its style and decoration. Small rooms were added to small rooms until the outside of the house, which is in parts rough cast, was a jumble of gables and imitation Tudor beams, and the inside a rabbit warren of small rooms. In many of these the overmantels are of a standard type which could be bought by the dozen and as Harold Nicolson has observed 'are indistinguishable from those of any Surbiton or Upper Norwood home'. Nor is the room in which five of Queen Mary's (who was then the Duchess of York, but will be referred to throughout as Queen Mary) children were born noticeably larger than the best bedroom would be in a house in one of these suburbs. Many years later the Duke of Windsor, writing about his father, said that, although he was a simple man, it was not true that he lived a simple life. Everything about him was always of the best, his clothes, his food, his guns; while perfection was expected in every detail of the service he received, whether at a banquet or at a shooting lunch. 'Nothing ever seemed to be forgotten; nothing ever seemed to go wrong.' Yet the Duke of Windsor also said: 'Until you have seen York Cottage you will never understand my father.' In spite of the fineness of his material possessions and the splendour of his entourage George v had undoubtedly a streak of eccentric simplicity of which York Cottage was the outward and visible sign.

He was a family man and for years he lived almost entirely at Sandringham, occupying his time with country pursuits, shooting and sailing, and also with his stamp collection. The physical comforts he demanded were by any standards low. The rooms at York Cottage as well as small were too few, the plumbing was primitive, and before meals the smell of cooking pervaded the air. When a third child was born, Princess Mary, she and her brothers shared one room by day and slept together with their nurse in one other by night. George v was entirely lacking in interest in matters of the intellect or arts. The pictures at York Cottage were reproductions, the furniture was supplied by Maples, and his own tiny study was covered in a red cloth intended for the trousers of French soldiers. The house spoke unequivocally of a narrow, indigent, but strongly individual taste.

Much has been written about the rigours of the lives of George v's children. Though he was a good and kind man, it is notorious that his relations with his sons were unhappy. The peculiar anxieties connected with the upbringing of royal children, particularly the heir to the throne, caused him, as it had caused his grandmother, to be constantly discontented with the objects of his concern. Very conservative by nature, he believed absolutely in the powers and benefits of discipline, although he himself as a young man was subject to uncontrollable fits of rage. These passed quickly, and were understood by his courtiers, but they made him very frightening to his sons. He has been defended against the charge of jealousy of the kind felt by the earlier Georges for their heirs but there seems, nevertheless, to have been an emotional quality in his feeling for his children, which no biographer has attempted to explain, but which made him irritable as well as anxious, hostile as well as affectionate. In addition, he was an unimaginative man and greatly given to 'chaff', a type of humour quite incomprehensible to children and often dreaded by them.

This might not have mattered so much if their mother had been able to protect them, if the circumstances of their lives had been different, or if they had been less nervous by temperament. George V was not so very different from many other fathers of his age. Chaffing was a popular manner of addressing children and it was a later generation that began to distinguish between the naughty and the inconvenient in the behaviour of the young. Queen Mary was not merely too shy and undemonstrative, but according to some accounts too much in awe of her husband herself, to be able to protect them against his wrath.

It was part of the upper-class system that children should depend not on their parents but on their nanny for the benefits of an intimate relationship. The barriers erected between children who were dressed up to see their parents and parents who received their children once a day were intensified in this family by the inevitable presence in the tiny drawing-room of the ladies-in-waiting. Finally, and almost unbelievably, the nanny who should have created a refuge from the terror of the outside world was, during Prince Albert's first years, a mentally unstable young woman with a preference for his elder brother, and she fed him so badly that he developed a chronic weakness of the stomach. When all this was discovered, she was replaced by the under-nurse Mrs Bill, after which stability could be counted on this nursery as in so many others.

Finally there were Grandpapa and Grandmama – King Edward VII and Queen Alexandra – who adored their grandchildren, gave them all the affection their own parents were unable to give and who encouraged them to be 'romps'. Children constantly berated on a system they cannot understand are inclined to react with an apparent indifference and a nervous boisterousness. A natural unruliness on the part of these royal children was so much encouraged by the King and Queen that their father, returning from a tour in Australia during which his sons had stayed with their grandparents, found them completely out of control. He therefore took them out of the care of Mrs Bill at the ages of seven-and-a-half and six respectively, and put them in charge of the nursery footman, Finch, who looked after them for the next eight years.

The three elder children – Princess Mary had been born in 1897 – were separated by some years from their young brothers and formed a little group of their own. Prince Albert is described as 'easily frightened and somewhat prone to tears'. He was also completely outshone by his elder brother whose dominance was one of the most important influences on his early life. Prince Edward (afterwards Edward VIII and Duke of Windsor) had according to almost everyone who ever knew him an extraordinary and magnetic charm. Beautiful and sad, yet responsive and gay, when he grew to manhood he could manipulate crowds or put individuals at ease with equal facility. For a few years he was one of the most popular princes in history. Yet no one felt his charms more strongly or admired him more unreservedly than the younger members of his family. They would have learned to revere him because he would be King but in the isolation of their lives – except on formal occasions they seldom met other children – he was not merely the most, he was almost the only attractive person they ever knew. Their profound feeling for him would grow and develop, and while in childhood they followed his leadership, as young men they ardently admired him.

With the possible exception of Prince George, Duke of Kent, all the children of George v and Queen Mary were of a highly nervous disposition. In Princess Mary the outward sign was an obvious shyness, in her two elder brothers it showed in nervous mannerisms. At the age of seven Prince Albert developed a stammer. This has sometimes been attributed to the fact that he was born left-handed and made to write with his right, but it was noticeable when he went to Osborne that, when he was with friends with whom he felt at ease, his stammer virtually disappeared. At other times it was of that obliterating kind which is almost as great a handicap as being blind or deaf. He had inherited the tendency to nervous rages characteristic of his family and suffered by both his father and his grandfather, and this was much intensified by his difficulty in speech. A further inheritance which caused him for a short time almost as much suffering was knock knees. To correct this he had to wear splints, which were so painful and wearisome that he was unable to do his lessons by day or sleep at night.

It is hardly surprising that this child should be given to 'outbursts of emotional excitement, sometimes of high spirits and exuberance, sometimes of passionate weeping and depression'. He is described as 'volatile' and 'mercurial' and it would be many years before he was able to control 'squalls of temper which, though of brief duration, left him exhausted in both body and mind'.

Nothing in his early education was designed to decrease this tension. When the time came to choose a tutor for his sons, their father's choice fell upon a gentleman named Hansell. George v gave more weight to good character than to book learning. Mr Hansell was a good golfer, a Norfolk man and a keen yachtsman, all characteristics which for his employer were inextricably mixed with moral virtue. In respect of moral virtue Hansell was worthy of the trust that was placed in him, he suffered only the disadvantage that he could not teach. In particular, he seems to have been unable to teach mathematics and both Prince Edward and Prince Albert were unable to master the rudiments of the subject. It was an essential part of the entrance examination to Osborne, to which both boys were destined. 'Despair would seize hold of him', Prince Albert's biographer writes, 'as problem after problem resisted his efforts to solve them and he would ultimately dissolve into angry tears.' And his father once wrote to him that he must really give up losing his temper when he made a small mistake in a sum.

The early life of these Princes was rich in ceremonial, full of the promptings of an exalted destiny – at the age of five Prince Albert stood with his brother to watch the burial of his great-grandmother and a few months later was present at the coronation of his grandfather, while from the earliest age he and his brother followed next

after their parents when they entered a room. Yet they lived in isolation from
their own generation, were starved of any real warmth or affection as well as of mental
and spiritual stimulus, while their family background, perhaps over full of temptation
to self-importance, was almost devoid of encouragement to a proper self-confidence.

All these things resulted in the most extraordinary performance when one after
the other reached Osborne. Prince Edward was to be congratulated when he reached
the position of 32nd in the term's order and Prince Albert was bottom at 71st and
caused very genuine relief to his tutors when at the end of his time at Dartmouth
he rose to 61st in a class of 67. At this time in his life he suffered from an almost
total inability to concentrate as well as nervous excitement, both more difficult to
overcome because of his stammer. Years later the Duke of Windsor used to say that
the only thing that saved him from his father's wrath was that, however badly he
did, his brother Bertie could be trusted to do worse. However, the Duke of Windsor
had by now become a little complacent about his intellectual failings and in retrospect
one is inclined to prefer a little honest rage.

One should not exaggerate the disadvantages under which these boys grew up.
They lived in an unpretentious but sincerely religious atmosphere. It was a part
of their parents' duty to go to church every Sunday, but they did this, not as a matter
of duty, but with a devout and unquestioning acceptance of the Christian faith. It
will be seen that nothing in the whole of his character or background would so sustain
the man who would one day be asked to pick up the burden and assume the duties,
as well as the rights, that his brother had laid down, as his strongly held religious
beliefs. Nor should it be forgotten that if he experienced the disadvantages of a disciplinary upbringing, he also received its advantages, as well as the inestimable benefits
of belonging to a family of good character and exceptional sense of duty.

➤

Then, too, the Princes lived in the country and learned to ride and fish and shoot.
Every year in the late summer they left Sandringham and went to the little castle
of Abergeldie at Balmoral. Nowhere in the world is more beautiful than Balmoral
with its hills and lochs and woods. Even the wild flowers have the brilliant colouring
of exotic plants and the changing skies have a translucent light no less enchanting
than the skies of Greece. Deer can be seen grazing by day as one passes along the
roads and at night their eyes glow in the darkness like fireflies. The castle of Abergeldie is as charming as any on the Rhine or in the Loire. As a child Prince Albert
spent every summer at Balmoral and he was there for some weeks when he was on
sick leave from the Navy. He grew to love it as no one since Queen Victoria had
loved it.

Both the Princes were very unhappy when they first went to Osborne. At all schools
new boys were subjected to some degree of bullying and Osborne had a particularly
restrictive disciplinary system and an emphasis on physical and mental hardness considered necessary for those who were being reared for the Navy. When one thinks

of the lives these particular children had led, the sense of privilege, the devoted attendants, their isolation, the shock they must have received is unimaginable.

There was much talk of the Princes being treated exactly the same as other boys but the truth is they were unable to meet their fellows on equal terms. Mr Hansell wrote to their father: 'They *must* have a certain amount of individual help and encouragement, especially encouragement, a too literal interpretation of the direction that they are to be treated exactly the same as other boys, who have had three or four years at a private school, must lead to disaster.' As they grew older the developing understanding of their fellows would also stand in the way of their being treated as other boys, but very young children have a minimum sense of homage or snobbery, and in their first year they did not escape the routine bullying.

In the long run Prince Albert did not merely settle down, he made friends at Osborne and Dartmouth. He shared with his elder brother one very charming attribute (which he also bequeathed to his daughters). When speaking to people he was what is called 'natural', a word not absolutely easy to define, although perfectly understood. It is a delightful characteristic, especially in members of the Royal Family, where it is unexpected. They do not condescend but nor do they seem constrained or conscious of any particular need for reserve. They are not affected, they talk in a straightforward way and are 'just the same as anyone else'. This candour, rarer than one might expect and attractive wherever it is met, accounted more than anything else for the depth of emotion the Prince of Wales would later inspire on his tours of the Empire. Prince Albert had none of the facility or brilliance of his brother, but he combined an open and friendly manner with a quality of kindness and consideration for others which won him affection from all who knew him well. His biographer tells the story of how when a group of cadets were invited by the owner of a small shoot to look at some pheasants, one of them who came from a modest urban background, provoked laughter by the remarks he made. It was Prince Albert who walked home with him and explained the technique of rearing and shooting birds. This might not be worth relating if it were not typical of stories that are told of him throughout his life. He was kind and considerate to others in an imaginatively sensitive way and he would go out of his way to protect people in potentially embarrassing situations.

Prince Albert, unlike his elder brother, was destined for a career in the Navy. When he joined the battleship *Collingwood*, for the first time in his life he left the shade cast by the other, and for the first time the often-repeated words came true and he was treated like any other newly appointed midshipman. He is said to have loved the Navy and the sea, although he had to fight a constant battle against seasickness. During the years of his service he grew to manhood, and during these years he proved that for all his backwardness and nervous temperament he could in practice be relied upon. So much secrecy surrounds the Royal Family and at the same time they are the objects of so much romantically inspired veneration that their real qualities often escape attention. Yet generation after generation of them possess certain dominant characteristics. They are extremely courageous and, in spite of lacking intellectual curiosity or attainments, they are often genuinely able.

Evelyn Waugh once said that courage was not a virtue but a necessary quality, and, while this may be a harsh standard for the rest of us, it is one required of the Royal Family. Prince Albert suffered for most of his years at sea from an undiagnosed duodenal ulcer which caused him great pain and resulted on several occasions in his being withdrawn from active service either to a hospital ship or on sick leave. He received much unpleasant and, as it turned out, ineffective treatment. One of these periods of pain and inaction took place in July 1915 when, in spite of being really ill, he could be persuaded to undertake treatment only on the assurance of the captain of his ship that, should the Fleet put to sea, he would be allowed to return to it. A correspondence which later took place between Captain Ley and King George V makes moving reading for the confidence with which the King spoke for his son. Captain Ley wrote that, although he had promised Prince Albert that he should be allowed to return to his ship if the Fleet put to sea, his doctor had said that it was inadvisable and might even be dangerous. He asked for instructions. Lord Stamfordham replied that the King attached the utmost importance to keeping faith with Prince Albert and said that the only possible alternative was to declare the Prince medically unfit, send him on sick leave and place him in a nursing home.

'This course His Majesty would however strongly deprecate ... even were the unexpected to happen and the Fleet were ordered to sea the day after you receive this letter, the King would prefer to run the risk of Prince Albert's health suffering than that he should endure the bitter and lasting disappointment of not being in his ship in the battle line.'

Another letter is interesting in the same connection. Lieutenant Campbell Tait, who, as well as being a friend of Prince Albert had become on friendly terms with the Prince of Wales during his visit to the ship, wrote to the latter to describe the occasion when the *Collingwood* put to sea for what was to become known as the battle of Jutland. Prince Albert, who for practical purposes had been given the sobriquet 'Mr Johnson', was on the sick list and in bed in an acute state of depression. 'Suddenly at about 2 p.m.', Lieutenant Campbell Tait wrote, 'a signal was received that the German High Seas Fleet was out and engaging our battle cruisers only forty miles away and that the battle was coming in our direction. Huge excitement. Out at last. Full speed ahead. Sound of "Action" – can you imagine the scene! Out of his bunk leaps "Johnson". Ill? Never felt better! Strong enough to go to his turret and fight a prolonged action. Of course he was, why ever not?'

'And', his biographer laconically remarks, 'to his turret he went, to remain there until the guns were firmly secured the next day.'

The Prince did well in the Navy, maintaining his position in spite of the constant illness which finally resulted in an operation to remove a duodenal ulcer, and being liked and trusted by all who came in contact with him. For evidence of his general ability one does not need to rely on the words of his commanding officers who might be trusted to gild the lily, because we have some of his letters as witness. His description of the *Collingwood*'s part in the battle of Jutland, for instance, is a simply written, factual but authoritative account of what he personally saw during twenty-four hours, and no word or phrase reminds us that the writer was accustomed to being 67th out of 67. It is very interesting to compare his letters to his parents at this stage in his career with those of the Prince of Wales. The elder brother's letters, to his friends as well as his parents, are noticeably schoolboyish in language, and those to his father almost invariably propitiatory in tone (possibly because he had so often ignored his father's instructions). Prince Albert's letters seem altogether more manly, and, although the King is always said to have been equally tyrannical with all his sons until after they married, they give the effect of being written to someone he loved and trusted. He even risked the occasional joke. Thus: 'On Friday night after I was turned in, I fell out of my hammock with the help of someone else, and hit my left eye on my chest. It swelled up very much and yesterday it was bandaged up.' To which the King replied: 'Sorry that with the help of someone else you fell out of yr. hammock and hit your eye on yr. chest ... I should do the same to the other fellow if I got the chance.'

The Prince had also a pronounced ability at games, and, like his brother and later his grand-daughter, he did not merely enter public events on equal terms with members of the public, he won them. At the end of 1917, having endured the operation for a duodenal ulcer which had for so long been necessary, he transferred, at his own request, from the Royal Navy to the Royal Navy Air Force. (The RAF was formed from the RNAS and the RFC in 1918.) Dr Louis Greig went with him. He had first met Dr Greig as a young medical officer when he was at Osborne and he met him again on his training cruise in the *Cumberland*. Greig (Group Commander Sir Louis Greig KBE, CVO) served with the Prince in 1917 and accompanied him as equerry when he transferred to the RNAS and later at Cambridge. He was his comptroller from 1920 to 1923 when he was Duke of York. Apart from the Prince's future wife, Greig probably exerted more influence on him than anyone else. He was a good athlete and an exceptionally good tennis player. He and the Prince would later win the RAF doubles together, the Prince was beaten only by Greig himself while in the semi-final of the singles in the same event. Helped, perhaps, by this partnership at games, Greig, who was an outspoken as well as an honest man, acted as guide, philosopher and friend. Too much (or so his early achievements both at work and at play seem to suggest) has been made of the Prince's nervous temperament, but when discouraged at games he would lose his temper as he had as a child at his sums. He sometimes stalked off the tennis court or a golf course in a rage, and, while it is impossible to distinguish between someone who is angry with himself for playing badly and someone who is a bad loser, both are equally embarrassing to the other players. Greig was in very close contact with the Prince, who lived in his house when he was in the Air Force and later at Cambridge, and he taught him the absolute necessity to control himself as well as the art of mixing with other people.

Both at Cranwell, where he was in charge of boys in training, and later at St Leonard's, where under Brigadier-General Critchley he had command of a squadron, the Prince proved himself to have inherited several of his father's qualities. He was dead keen and he was something of a martinet, having like his father a belief in discipline and a desire for smartness which made him a good if slightly insensitive commander. When the King visited his base at St Leonard's he was frankly delighted with him.

In October 1918, at the eleventh hour before victory, the Prince was posted to General Trenchard's staff and flew the Channel with Louis Greig to report to RAF headquarters at Antigny. He was in time to witness operations for day and night bombing by the English, American, Italian and French air forces. At the end of the war he transferred to the staff of Major-General Sir John Salmond and he remained with the armies in France or Belgium until the following spring. During this period he for the first time represented his father on a matter of state, accompanying the King of the Belgians on his official entry into Brussels. He also applied to Sir John Salmond for permission to fly, securing his and later the King's approval for this project.

Prince Albert did not care for flying but he felt that if he was to remain in the Air Force he must earn his wings. His instruction took place partly in France and partly, on his return to England, at Croydon. The good co-ordination which he had already shown as a tennis player and his keenness and determination enabled him to learn to fly and to do acrobatics as well as cross-country flying. When he would normally have flown solo for the first time, his medical examiners advised that his general physical and psychological condition was not good enough for him to do so, although it seems more likely that at this stage in the history of flying no one would take the risk. In any case, his instructor accompanied him on his tests, sitting with his hand on the bottom of the struts but not touching the controls. King George VI was the only member of the Royal Family to become a fully qualified pilot.

In July 1919 it was decided that Prince Albert should return to civilian life and rather unexpectedly his father decided that he should go with his brother Prince Henry for a few terms to Trinity, Cambridge. Prince Albert studied history, economics and civics, being particularly interested in the development of the constitution. Unlike his grandfather and his elder brother, both he and Prince Henry seemed seriously anxious to learn. 'Their freshness and willingness to learn made for a very pleasant relationship between tutor and pupil, and all who came in contact with them ... were delighted with their naturalness and friendliness.'

In 1920 the King conferred on Prince Albert the title Duke of York which he had borne himself. When the Duke came down from Cambridge he divided his normal working hours between the routine duties of the Royal Family and the work of the Industrial Welfare Society which was his special interest. He had been asked to become President of the Boys' Welfare Association before he went up to Cambridge, and with the King's approval he accepted. This Association, which soon developed into the Industrial Welfare Society, known today as the Industrial Society, deserves some attention both for its own sake and because his connection with it was to be of absorbing interest to the Duke until he became King, as well as his major contribution to public life.

In 1916 Seebohm Rowntree drew the attention of Lloyd George (then in charge of the Ministry of Munitions) to the total inadequacy of the arrangements for women and boys drafted into the factories during the war, and Lloyd George responded by asking him to set up a Welfare Advisory Department within the Ministry itself. Rowntree recruited a man called Robert Hyde to run the section dealing with the employment of boys. He found the red tape of a government office too thwarting, and left in 1918 to found the Boys' Welfare Association. In 1919 this became the Industrial Welfare Association.

From the start the Society had hard, explicit aims, and should not be confused with the many well-intentioned and often beneficial movements launched during the depression after the war with the vaguer aim of relieving the unhappiness caused by poverty and unemployment, the exact impact of which it is difficult now to assess. It was founded with the direct intention of improving conditions for workers in industry, and there was plenty for it to do in an age when it was possible to find a factory which had only one lavatory for 90 women and another where women were paid $1\frac{1}{2}$d for 80 buttons and holes and fined 2d if they missed one, where contributory pension and educational schemes were virtually unknown, and sports clubs and canteens hardly even thought of. It was of the greatest importance to find a President with sufficient prestige to influence public opinion and particularly employers and to help in the raising of funds. Hyde also felt that it was desirable for a member of the Royal Family to learn something of the industrial life of the country. No choice could have been more propitious than that of the Duke of York. He developed a serious interest in the work and played an active part. Embarking at once on a series of visits to industrial centres, he insisted there should be no ceremonial and that conditions should be normal when he toured factories. It is obvious that his keen interest would have enormously influenced employers and pleased the workers. He was also active in raising funds.

Out of his relationship with the Industrial Society, there grew an annual event, even more personal to himself, which became known as the Duke of York's Camp. He was very much attracted to an idea suggested to him by Sir Alexander Grant (who was also prepared to donate finance) that much good could be done if boys from public schools and from industry could be brought together for leisure occupations on terms of equality. It was the Duke himself who thought of the idea of a camp and with his usual enthusiasm he immediately put the scheme into effect. One hundred public schools and one hundred industrial firms were invited to send two boys each to meet and mix with each other as the Duke's guests for a week's holiday camp on terms of complete equality. After the success of the first camp it was decided to make it an annual event.

In the light of the very different circumstances and attitudes of today it is difficult to be sure how much resulted from these camps, but among the certain gains was a great deal of enjoyment for a great many people (among whom must be numbered the Duke himself); while one must assume that, even if the boys from the factories had little to gain from their meeting with the public school boys, the latter must have gained in understanding from their meetings with them.

So much for the Duke's public life. In private he spent much of his leisure at Sandringham and Balmoral. He was a good horseman and he enjoyed hunting with the Pytchley but shooting was his first love and would remain so all his life. In the summer of 1920 at a small dance given by Lord Farquhar he met Lady Elizabeth Bowes-Lyon.

TWO

LADY ELIZABETH BOWES-LYON

L ADY ELIZABETH BOWES-LYON, born on 4 August 1900, was the ninth child of the Earl of Strathmore. There was an interval of seven years after the birth of five elder brothers and three sisters before her own, but a younger brother, David, was born in 1902. This family was as happy, warm and loving as it was large, and there is an immediate temptation to contrast the childhood of the girl he was to marry with the deprived and handicapped youth of the Duke of York. There was one thing common to the environment of both, however, which was as important as it was rare.

Lady Elizabeth came of a family which could trace its descent in a direct line from the fourteenth century and like her future husband she was a descendant of Robert Bruce through his grandson King Robert II. At Glamis Castle in Forfarshire, in a countryside of no less beauty, if less heroic, than at Balmoral, she must early have become aware of a noble past stretching beyond the Hanoverians and the Stuarts to medieval times; for just as few families can boast such unbroken descent, so few castles with the long past of Glamis are still lived in. It is on the site of an eleventh-century hunting lodge, the oldest parts date from the fifteenth century, the rest from the early seventeenth. Dorothy Laird has already made the point that of all the royal homes in which the future Queen would live, only Windsor Castle and the Palace of Holyrood can compare in tradition with Glamis. Mary, Queen of Scots, stayed there, so did Prince Charlie, while there is a legend that Shakespeare set the murder of King Duncan by Macbeth in the original guardroom of the castle, now named Duncan's Hall.

The Bowes-Lyon family lived at Glamis only for the late months of the summer and early autumn, except during the Great War, when Lady Elizabeth and her parents spent some years there. At all other times they lived at St Paul's, Waldenbury, in Hertfordshire and this they regarded as home. St Paul's is all that most people imagine when they think of an English country house and any description of it is full of evocative words. It was built of red brick in the reign of Queen Anne and magnolia grows on its walls. In the garden there are green paths between pleached trees and a star-shaped wood, attributed to Le Notre, which, because of its converging rides, gives the illusion of being part of a forest. All round is the farmland and, while in the house in those days there were still-rooms and laundry-rooms and dairies, outside there were barns and lofts and harness rooms and stalls where the ponies stood. All were filled with human beings whose purpose in life was to serve this family.

The Bowes-Lyon children, like the royal children, were brought up in a religious belief deeply and devoutly held, a part of their natural heritage. Lady Strathmore taught her two younger children herself. 'At the age of 6 & 7,' David Bowes-Lyon wrote, 'we each could have written a fairly detailed account of all the Bible stories.' As in the case of the boy she would marry, one cannot over-emphasize the importance of her religious faith in all the crises of the future Queen's life.

Here, however, all comparison between the two families ends, because, although in both the children were taught the obligations of their rank and possessions, Prince Albert struggled to understand the precepts of his inarticulate father – who adjured his children not to 'think themselves better than anyone else' – while Lady Elizabeth imbibed it in the air she breathed.

Lady Strathmore was a very remarkable woman and, in days when the children of most upper-class homes were brought up in the nursery and merely on visiting terms with their parents, she spent her life surrounded by her numerous brood. She had an extraordinary zest for life and was both musical and skilful in the decorative arts. When the bedstead on which Prince Charlie had slept at Glamis, elaborately worked in many coloured silks on orange satin, wore out, Lady Strathmore copied it exactly and under the valance embroidered the names of each of her children. As well as stories of the Bible, she taught her two younger children – Elizabeth and David, whom she called her two Benjamins – the rudiments of music, dancing and drawing. She was not a disciplinarian (indeed she was so casual that on one occasion being told by a guest that water was running down her drawing-room wall, she remarked that the sofa beneath it ought to be moved) but she maintained that effortless authority which comes from unquestioning certainty about the moral and spiritual virtues. This quality, perhaps more than any other, impressed itself on the developing character of her youngest daughter.

Here is a description of St Paul's, Waldenbury, written by a friend of the family:

'There was a beautiful garden ready to be enjoyed, and plenty of work always waiting to be done in it. There were dogs to be looked after and chickens to be fed. There was a tennis court out of doors and a much-used piano within. There was no extravagance or luxury; no attempt to be modern or up-to-date.... Yet if there be a genius for family life, it was surely found in that household.'

Lady Elizabeth inherited many of her mother's qualities and these were of a kind best fostered in the environment in which she was born. People speak of her dignity and courtesy, her desire to be pleasant to others from the youngest age. She was never shy and she had a quiet and natural confidence which gave her the air of being entirely at home wherever she happened to be. Above all, she was born with what Voltaire called '*le grand art de plaire*'. Lord Gorell in a letter to Lady Cynthia Asquith said:

> 'In the simplest and most unconscious way she was all-conquering. In addition to the charm of especially winsome childhood, she had, even then, that blend of kindness and dignity that is peculiar to her family. She was small for her age, responsive as a harp, wistful and appealing one moment, bright-eyed and eager the next, with a flashing smile of appreciative delight ... quick of intelligence, alive with humour, able to join in any of the jokes and hold her own with the jokers, and touchingly and sometimes amusingly loyal to her friends.'

While another correspondent wrote:

> 'Elizabeth was always the most astonishing child for knowing the right thing to say. All agree as to the remarkable tact shown in early childhood. Had she been consciously rehearsing for her future she could scarcely have practised her manners more assiduously: but then, as now, their excellence was due, not to the desire to win praise, but to the instinct to make others comfortable.'

And finally Lady Cynthia herself:

> 'Those who knew the Duchess [written when Queen Elizabeth was Duchess of York] tell me the promise of the flower was discernible in the bud and that it was almost as though she had a premonition of her destiny and was rehearsing for the part she was one day to play.'

She was early nicknamed Princess Elizabeth and she liked this name and used it about herself. This was not necessarily a portent. In those days Princesses had not only the smallest feet and the fairest faces, they stopped their carriages to give aid to passers-by while their sisters swept on; they alone gave food to old women who called at the door; and they instantly detected a pea beneath the mattress. She liked dressing up, too, and grand clothes, and this, if not a portent, was at least a happy circumstance in view of the life she was later to lead.

Some of the sayings of the little Princess have the oddest ring today. Thus at the age of three to a factor on the estate: 'How do you do, Mr Ralston. I haven't seen you look so well, not for years and years, but I am sure you will be sorry to know that Lord Strathmore has got the toothache.' Like all the children of the landed nobility, she was brought up in an entirely paternalistic society.

Yet if attitudes have changed, human nature has not, and it is the degree of engagement and desire to please shown to Mr Ralston that has enabled Queen Elizabeth,

Above King George VI aged two years.
Below Queen Elizabeth as a child.

Left Lady Elizabeth Bowes-Lyon with her father the Earl of Strathmore.

Below Glamis Castle, the home of the Strathmore family since 1372. The main part of the castle is now open to the public and the present Earl of Strathmore and his family occupy one wing.

Opposite Lady Elizabeth Bowes-Lyon aged fourteen.

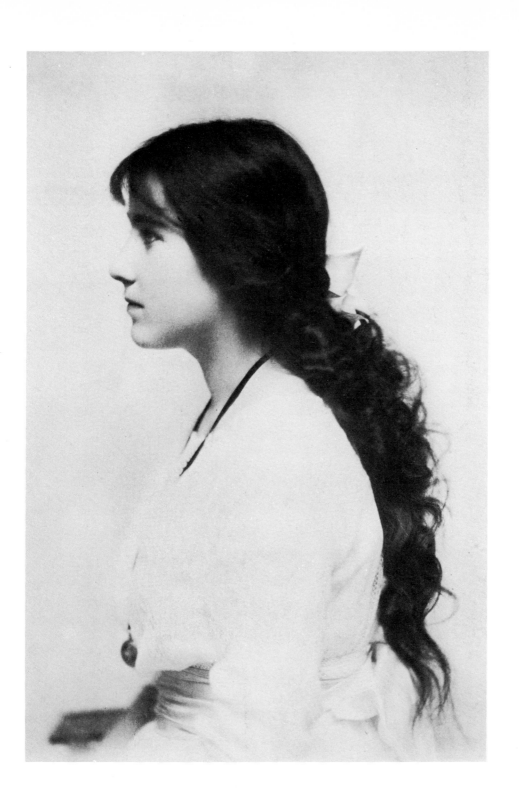

Opposite The royal children. Princess Mary is standing between her elder brother, Prince Edward (on her left), and her second brother, Prince Albert. In front Prince Henry is standing between his brother, Prince George (on his left), and the youngest child, Prince John, who died in 1919 at the age of fourteen.

Right Queen Mary, then Princess of Wales, with Prince Edward (on her left) and Prince Albert at Abergeldie in 1906.

Below Sandringham.

Prince Albert, Duke of York.

Lady Elizabeth Bowes-Lyon.

The Duke of York and Lady Elizabeth Bowes-Lyon at the time of their engagement in 1922.

without in the least endangering 'the mystery and the magic', to go beyond the role of modern royalty and give genuine comfort to others.

As a little girl she had a passion for cake. 'May I come in,' she asked a member of her mother's household, 'and eat more – *much* more – of that chocolate cake than I liked to eat while it was upstairs?' Yet an entry in her diary shows a subtle combination of strong opinion and self-control which must be interesting to those who know her well today. 'Some governesses are nice,' it reads, 'some *are not.*'

The Strathmores, like other members of the landed nobility, had a house in London (in 21 St James's Square) but their children's lives were spent almost entirely in the country. Lady Elizabeth had a pony called Bobs and two pigs, Lucifer and Emma, hens that insisted on laying their eggs in a place called the Flea House, bantams, tortoises and cats. In the early summer she went haymaking, and often she was up and out at six o'clock in the morning. All her life she was on easy terms with country people and all her life she naturally took part in country pursuits.

In the war she went with her parents to Glamis Castle, which was turned into a military hospital for convalescents, and between the ages of fourteen and eighteen she saw more of human suffering and endurance than many people see in a lifetime. Here she first showed that single-minded interest in people, found in the best doctors, teachers and social workers, which enabled her to concentrate her attention entirely on the man or woman she was with. She amused and comforted the patients, playing games with them and writing their letters, above all establishing a genuine relationship. Thomas Hardy quotes Pascal as saying: '*A mesure qu'on a plus d'esprit on trouve qu'il y a plus d'hommes originaux. Les gens communs ne trouvent pas de différence entre les hommes.*' Someone seeking the key to Queen Elizabeth's career might find it in these words.

Yet it cannot be said too soon or too often that what has distinguished her throughout her life from many people of like temperament is that, entirely serious in purpose, she is invariably light-hearted in approach. She suffers not from self-pity, that most moving and enervating of emotions, and, since she is capable of great feeling, she is never under the necessity of assuming it. She has responded to all the moments of crisis in her own career with the light and under-stated answer.

In 1918 she was young and recuperative and she had great powers of enjoyment, and, in the aftermath of the war, when the great London houses began to re-open and aristocratic society to return to the ways of peace, she followed the routine of the debutante as eagerly as any other girl. She was pretty and gay and she had the immeasurable opportunities to meet others of her own age, afforded only to the young, and of her own social class.

When she married the Duke of York it was a matter of personal choice. She hesitated for nearly two years because she knew that to marry a member of the Royal Family was forever to put behind her whole areas of personal freedom and the liberty to form personal relationships which the rest of us take for granted. She was too intelligent and too conscientious not to know that for her this marriage would mean renunciation of much that is really valuable in life, as well as total dedication to an ideal and an institution. Most young girls fear the commitment which marriage involves – in marriage to a member of the Royal Family this commitment is absolute.

Why then did she choose it? It is often said that she alone recognised the real worth of this shy and stammering youth, while we are constantly told of his nervous temperament. Yet he was very good-looking – he was fleet of foot and had particularly good physical co-ordination. He was matured by experience of the war. He must have shone in the country-house atmosphere of tennis, shooting and riding. Then he was so keen, trying exceptionally hard and seriously at everything he undertook, a quality which Lady Elizabeth shared and must have liked. The truth is he was a private person and had little to contribute to the social scene, but as a private person he had two exceptional characteristics. The first, as we have already seen, was the quality of his kindness, which was to win him devoted friends all his life and must have been irresistible to the woman he loved. The other, less obvious, was that his modesty was so innate, his vanity so little, that having all his life been outshone by his brother, he now chose a partner whose social talents were no less.

One of Lady Elizabeth's friends said to Cynthia Asquith: 'I daresay she was very much afraid of the position but she just found she couldn't do without him.' Maybe, or maybe she found he could not do without her. It is more blessed to give than to receive, but it is equally necessary to most people. In hindsight when one looks back on the careers of these two, they seem wonderfully complementary to each other, yet at this time because of the difference in their birth and upbringing, she had so much to offer, while he was so much in need.

He had one thing to offer her, however, even though she may not have been conscious of it. This was a role large enough for her gifts. In any walk of life she would have made full use of these gifts, but where else on such a scale? One can imagine many other things she might have done, but all are diminished by what she did do. She cannot have been entirely cold to her opportunity.

THREE

THE YORKS

IT WAS THOUGHT very delightful that the Yorks were so happy and succeeded in living a full private life. There is something a little chilling about the arranged royal marriage, and it is not until years of habit have coupled the partners to it in the public mind that it is possible for the ordinary person to identify with them. The Yorks so young and so obviously in love gave great satisfaction both to the public and the Royal Family.

King George v's behaviour to his sons changed completely once they were married, when he was released from the carping anxiety about their welfare and their conduct which had so damaged their relationship with him. In the case of the Duke of York he must have been much influenced by his desire not to upset his daughter-in-law, whom he found irresistible. 'Unlike his own children, I was never afraid of him,' she wrote after his death, 'and in all the twelve years of having me as a daughter-in-law he never spoke one unkind or abrupt word to me.'

The Duchess of York was by nature unpunctual, a failing which arose largely through her concentration on the person she was with or the thing she was doing at any one moment, and one which increased considerably over the years as she grew more authoritative and more able to do as she pleased. King George v on the other hand regarded unpunctuality as a vice and even the Prince of Wales tore strips off the tyres of his car in his efforts not to provoke his father on this score. Yet, when one of his Household remarked on the unpunctuality of his daughter-in-law, the King sprang to her defence, remarking that if she were not sometimes late she would be perfect, which would be horrible. 'You are indeed a lucky man to have such a charming & delightful wife as Elizabeth,' he wrote to his son. And: 'The better I know and the more I see of your dear little wife, the more charming I think she is & everyone feels in love with her here.'

Queen Mary, too, was very pleased with her daughter-in-law. As a young woman she had often been made unhappy by Queen Alexandra who, always represented as so sunny in temperament, had a possessive love for her sons which made her difficult in the role of mother-in-law. Possibly with these memories in mind, Queen Mary was invariably kind and considerate to her son's wife. The Duchess of York did not need to establish relations with her brother-in-law, the Prince of Wales, because she had known him since, as a debutante, she had met him in the London ballrooms. 'He was such fun,' she would say regretfully many years later.

When they were first married the Yorks were lent White Lodge in Richmond Park, where Queen Mary had lived as a girl and where the Prince of Wales had been born. Originally simply one of many lodges in Richmond Park and today the home of the Royal Ballet School, White Lodge stands in the middle of the Park and was much enlarged by a daughter of George II. It has a beautiful garden and a tennis court and the Yorks enjoyed one summer there. But it was too big and expensive to run and above all too far from the centre of London. In winter it was often lost in fog and in too many ways it was unsuitable for the life they had to lead. They soon began to look for a more convenient house as a permanent home and their choice fell on 145 Piccadilly (which stood at Hyde Park Corner but which no longer exists) although they did not move into this until the following year after their return from a tour in Australia. Several years later the King gave them the Royal Lodge in Windsor Park.

None of these houses can be described as in any way like those of the ordinary young married couple, but inside the flower-laden rooms the Yorks contrived a life which had all the warmth and gaiety of the happiest of their contemporaries and as little as possible of the formality of a palace. They chose the gentlemen and ladies-in-waiting from among their most intimate friends.

The Duchess seemed to find no difficulty in undertaking her new duties. If she were shy or nervous, she did not show it and it is doubtful whether she ever was. She had far more experience of meeting people and of semi-public duties than most girls of her age, and the warmth of her interest in everything she did entirely engaged her mind. Her popularity quickly became second only to that of the Prince of Wales himself. There was a similarity in their public manner. The Prince, too, was beloved for his ability to treat a crowd as a number of separate individuals worthy of his attention and between them they set a new fashion for modern royalty. Only the years would show that what in him was a youthful ardour easily exhausted was in her a natural instinct and a matter of deep conviction.

She did not outshine the Prince, nor did she wish for more than a purely secondary role but she performed her public duties with obvious enjoyment. To everything she was required to do, she constantly added causes which were personally dear to her, and from the beginning she resisted all attempts by her staff to limit her interests or reduce the physical strain upon her. She suffered only one disadvantage for her public role. She does not photograph well and like many women with a beautiful skin and complexion, she is far prettier in the flesh than she appears from the photographs which appear in the press.

Socially she was regarded as very charming and amusing. She is a natural mimic (a quality both her daughters have inherited) and it is natural to her to drop into the accent or idiom of people who crop up in her speech. The Yorks did not, as the Prince of Wales did, join that set of young married people who were so often to be seen in night-clubs, but they lived a very full life with only minor restraints on their freedom to do as they pleased.

When on 21 April 1926 Princess Elizabeth was born, although she replaced the Duke of Gloucester as third in succession to the throne, the true importance of the occasion was not recognised because it was still believed that it was only a question of time before the Prince of Wales would himself make a suitable marriage. Nor had it as yet been suggested that when two young people of the royal blood become the parents of a third, they satisfy the deep primeval longing of mankind for an ideal family. On tour in Australia in the following year both Princess Elizabeth's parents were to be taken by surprise by the intensity of the interest in her. 'It is extraordinary how her arrival is so popular out here,' the Duke wrote to his mother. 'Wherever we go cheers are given for her as well & the children write to us about her.' In England the opportunities to express this interest had so far been less, but it was equally strong as events would prove.

Much less was known about the new baby than would have been today. Without the competition of television, newspaper reporters were less importunate. As late as 1936 it was possible for Harold Nicolson to write to his wife that he had sat down next to the Duchess of York with only the vaguest feeling that she was somehow familiar, until someone came into the room and dropped her a curtsey. But: 'She is charm personified,' he reported.

As a result the first years of the future Queen were not different in any important respect from those of the first born in more ordinary families of the land. It was not merely that her birth gave her parents all the normal satisfactions of such occasions (although to the Duke particularly, who had hardly known such delights were part of the human heritage, it brought unexpected happiness) but that the Duchess of York broke away, as her mother had before her, from the conventions of her class. In an age when the system by which upper-class children were brought up was designed, by creating artificial barriers between parents and their young, to stultify natural parental emotions, Princess Elizabeth and later Princess Margaret Rose knew no barrier between the nursery and the rest of the house, nothing of the restrictive atmosphere of the dressed-up daily meeting in the drawing-room. Mrs Dudley Ward once boasted that 'hers was the first house without a green baize door'. At 145 Piccadilly the Duchess of York might have said almost the same. Toys were to be found in all the main rooms of the house, shrieks of laughter could be heard from the Duchess's rooms in the mornings, and, as the children grew up, their ease and freedom in adult society was a constant source of wonder to their father. 'We used to be so shy,' he often said. The future sovereign of England grew up in the secure environment of a united, openly demonstrative, stable and loving family. Of what other sovereign in all history can the same be said?

►

We have been told of the peculiar trials of the stammerer, of the enraging inability ever to contribute the spontaneous witticism or correct the obvious error, to support a friend or confound an enemy. It is not only that the occasion too often passes by but the pain and embarrassment of the interrupted delivery are too great to be easily undertaken. Chips Channon described the Duke of York as 'good, dull, dutiful and good-natured' and no one who did not know him well could say that this was not an adequate description of him.

This might not have seemed very important to the Duke himself, since he had no desire to shine on the social scene, if he had not been a hard, ambitious worker, confined by his inheritance to one kind of work. As we have seen, he developed a sphere of his own in industrial welfare and with his boys' camp, but in the main his duties were to represent the King, and at this time these were much increased by the frequent absence of the Prince of Wales from England. One can think of no greater handicap or more constant humiliation for a member of the Royal Family than to stutter.

The Duke's difficulties came to a head when Stanley Bruce, the High Commissioner for Australia, requested King George to send one of his sons to perform the ceremony of opening the legislative buildings in the new capital of Canberra in 1927. The King thought it particularly appropriate to send his second son, since, as Duke of York, he had himself opened the first session of the Dominion Government in Melbourne on one of the earliest of the royal world tours. He was naturally hesitant because of the Duke's speech, while for the same reason Mr Bruce, when it was suggested, was openly appalled. It was at about this time, however, that the Duke was induced to consult a speech therapist called Lionel Logue. He had previously tried one treatment after another without result and had begun to feel 'the inconsolable despair of the chronic stammerer and the secret dread that the hidden root of his affliction lay in the mind rather than in the body'. When he entered Logue's consulting room the latter described him as 'a slim, quiet man, with tired eyes and all the outward symptoms of the man upon whom habitual speech defect had begun to set the sign'.

Logue's method was to treat both the psychological and the physical difficulties in the way of normal speech, first giving his patient confidence that he could be cured and then teaching him to breathe properly. The method was based, much as the art of acting or singing is based, on breathing at the appropriate moment and sufficiently to sustain the line of the sentence. When the Duke's public speeches were prepared, trouble had to be taken to see that the sentences were of the best length. He almost immediately made progress and within a month wrote to his father: 'I wish I could have found him before, as now that I know the right way to breathe my fear of talking will vanish.' This was a slightly optimistic estimate. The Duke's fear and hatred of talking, at any rate in public, would never entirely vanish. The improvement was great and sufficient to allow him to carry out his public duties, but to the end of his life he seemed to the sensitive listener to ride his speech as a man rides a bad-tempered horse, by skill, knowledge and patience but also by faith. All would be well as long as his nerve held. On their Australian tour, it first became obvious to the onlooker to what an extent his wife encouraged his faith.

She had taken great interest in his treatment, several times visiting Logue's consulting rooms herself, and learning to help her husband with the breathing exercises. But it was the unspoken communication between them that so struck all those who watched. In the terrible difficulties of his task he seemed to be sustained not merely by his own strength, which was not wanting, but also by hers. Onlookers have described how he would sometimes turn and look at her across a room and how, when he did this, she left what she was doing and went immediately to his side; he then seemed enabled to carry on. Nor was it only the Duke she inspired with confidence but also those who heard him. When she sat on a platform beside him, no trace of anxiety or doubt ever disturbed the smiling serenity of her bearing; by no flicker of her features did she betray concern if he stumbled or hesitated. No one knew what passed through her mind but she transmitted a sense of ease to the crowds who listened as well as to the man who spoke. 'Not only did the Queen have all the courage in the world,' one of her Household was later to say, 'she had the power to transmit it to you.'

The Duke and Duchess of York left Portsmouth for Australia on 6 January 1927. Among the Duke's staff were Surgeon-Commander H. E. Y. White and Lieutenant Commander Colin Buist, both of whom had been at Dartmouth with him, and among the Duchess's, Lady Cavan and Mrs Gilmour, of whom one of the Duchess's earlier biographers has said that she was not only a close personal friend 'but very efficient'. She has remained a close personal friend ever since.

The tour was a magnificent success. All royal tours are successful and it is only from a subjective point of view that there is much real anxiety on this score. Their importance to the biographer is often less for the impact of the royal personage on the cheering crowds than for the impact of the crowds on him. Several features of this tour distinguish it from any other, and it was of undoubted importance in the development of the future King and Queen.

It was notable to begin with for the instant and overwhelming impact made by the Duchess of York. Much has already been said of her private and public charms but this was her first appearance on the world stage and her first opportunity to display the range and scope of her talents for this particular role. In almost every aspect of a royal life the Duke had to overcome physical or mental disabilities, but the Duchess was blessed with all the natural advantages. In a small, prosaic but important way this was demonstrated as soon as the *Renown*, on which they travelled (and which had also carried the Prince of Wales on most of his tours) met high seas. We have already seen that the Duke of York had to struggle all his life with seasickness, but the Duchess was a born traveller. 'I have never known her upset by a train, a car, a boat or an aeroplane: she's impervious,' one of her ladies-in-waiting would say many years later. And she added: 'One can hardly imagine a more useful quality for Royalty.'

The Duke and Duchess visited New Zealand on their way to Australia, and, during the course of an almost impossibly heavy schedule of receptions, dinners, balls, garden-parties and official visits, gave instant and lasting pleasure to their hosts and learned confidence in themselves. It was here they began to develop the almost telepathic understanding between them which has already been referred to and which was the most remarkable feature of their lives together and of their public appearances.

In March, after they had completed their tour of the North Island and reached Christchurch, the Duchess developed tonsillitis and was compelled to return to Government House at Wellington. At the time this was regarded as a major disaster, particularly by the Duke, who, believing that she was the main attraction to the crowds, was dismayed and distressed at having to carry on without her. It has since been agreed that the warmth of his welcome when he did so was the turning point in his career. Better at games and a better horseman than his elder brother, on leisure occasions he won liking and respect for his sportsmanship; in public he was carried along by the enthusiasm of the crowds. All this gave him confidence, even enthusiasm, for the far more difficult task of speaking at the opening of the Parliament at Canberra. When the royal coupled reached Australia, the Duchess now completely recovered, they passed from state to state in what has been described as 'a blaze of ecstasy'. 'I don't believe such a scene could have been reproduced anywhere outside the Empire,' the Governor reported, 'and I am certain that nothing could have given rise to it except a royal visit.'

There were two precedents for the extraordinary demonstrations that met the Duke and Duchess wherever they went. The first was the tours of George v, when Duke of York, in Australia and, as Prince of Wales, in India; the second the tours of the Duke's elder brother, the Prince of Wales, throughout the Empire – far more recent and among the most spectacularly successful public occasions in history.

George v had returned from each of his tours in a spirit of awe. He had been overwhelmed by the emotions of the crowds wherever he went. 'It was forced upon him', his biographer writes, 'that nothing had contributed so much to produce those unmistakable manifestations of loyalty and love of England as the life and example of Queen Victoria . . . She was the first British monarch whose character and personal influence had suggested the idea of the Throne as a symbol of Imperial Unity.' And in India: 'He saw then the extent to which the whole Empire might stand or fall by the personal example set from the throne, and to insure the integrity of that example he was to sacrifice much that men hold dear, much that makes life sweet.'

The Prince of Wales, on the other hand, who travelled as a much younger man and one of oustanding personal charm and public skill, had in the long run become

THE WEDDING DAY, 26 APRIL 1923
The Wedding Group included the Earl and Countess of Strathmore and King George V and Queen Mary. The carriage is carrying the Duke and Duchess of York away from Buckingham Palace after the reception.

On their honeymoon at Polesdon Lacy near Dorking in Surrey.

The Duchess of York at a coconut shy in 1923 during an outing at Loughton for the Fresh Air Fund.

The Duke of York taking part in the Men's Doubles Championships at Wimbledon in 1926.

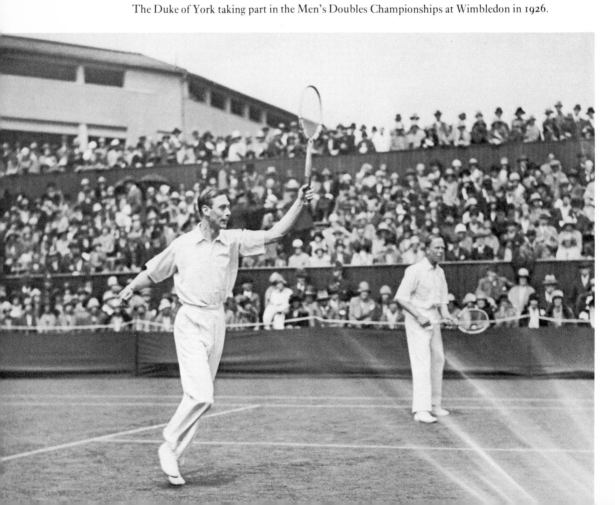

The Duchess catches a trout during a fishing expedition at Takaanu in New Zealand in 1925.

The Duke and Duchess visit a factory in the Midlands in 1925.

The Duke of York with General Baden-Powell watching a Scout Jamboree at Wembley in 1924.

The Yorks arriving at Skye in 1933.

King Edward VIII and Mrs Simpson: in a London nightclub
and (*below*) during a holiday in Europe.

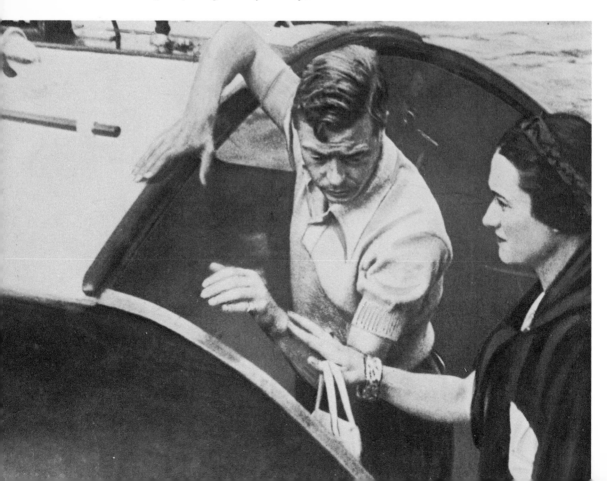

satiated by success, tired of the everlasting planting of trees and laying of foundation stones, weary of the eternal demands on his good humour, disillusioned by the need to remain, in his own words, 'a wayfarer rather than a sojourner' and the necessity, once he had begun to establish personal relationships with people and things, to move on. It seems likely that he attached too much weight to his own contribution to the success of the tours and too little to the far more solid and lasting appeal of the Crown as an institution – and this is not entirely surprising in view of the real quality of the former. Nevertheless, whereas his father's biographers have no doubt that King George V's character was moulded and fired in the heat of his reception in the Empire, the same experience wore out his son's stock of ardour and left him bored and emotionally unresponsive to the crowds.

In 1927 the Duke of York was very pleased with his success and with his own achievements – pardonably proud that he had surmounted the real difficulties of the tour. But he had met the experience with awe and an awakening sense of his own responsibilities, as his father had before him, with 'a new vision of Empire' and his duties towards it. If one were to attempt to account for the continuing life of the monarchical principle in England, it seems hardly too much to say that it owes more than anything else to the fact that, in the face of these massive demonstrations of love and loyalty, three out of four of the ruling sovereigns of the House of Windsor have been capable of a sense of humility.

One further thing in connection with this tour must be recorded. When the *Renown* reached Portsmouth on its return voyage, the Prince of Wales came on board to welcome his brother and sister-in-law home. He was no doubt pleased to see them and it was the *Renown* which had carried him on his own tours a few years before. It may be possible for posterity to doubt whether the Prince's personal magnetism would have seemed so overpowering to such a variety of people if he had not been royal. What is not open to question is the extraordinary skill he displayed for public and semi-public occasions, the pleasure he gave by his gift of recognising immediately men he had not seen for several years, his talent for the well-chosen word, or the vividness of the smile which lit his sad little face. The Duke of York had won approval over the months for his hard work, his dignity and his goodness, but now he was in the presence of a master. In an hour or two on the *Renown* the Prince of Wales gave a virtuoso performance which would never be forgotten by those who saw it.

✦

Princess Margaret was born in 1930 and in 1931 the King gave the Duke of York Royal Lodge in Windsor Park – thus was joy compounded. Observers have said that the Duke was always aware of his elder daughter's seriousness of purpose, intellect and character and that he loved her unreservedly. By Princess Margaret Rose, he was bewitched. She was a really beautiful child, whose eyes, which are large, dark blue and soft but stare at one with a not uncritical sparkle, express her character. As a young girl she was small, slender and elegant. She was quick-witted and musically gifted and she had inherited her mother's talent for mimicry which she put to spirited use. The Duke could not take his eyes off her, but he looked at her with an air of disbelief, as one might who, with no pretensions himself, had sired a changeling sprite.

The Royal Lodge ('I hope you will always call it *the* Royal Lodge', George v wrote to his son, 'by which name it has been known ever since George iv built it', but probably because it is not natural to use 'the' his son seems not to have obeyed him), was originally built partly by Nash and partly by Wyatville to the order of their extravagant client and then largely demolished by William iv. In 1931 it consisted chiefly of a great saloon of Wyatville's design and a charming octagonal room built on to the end of it by Queen Adelaide and hung inside with chintz in the manner of a marquee. Wyatville's great unfinished saloon had been roofed by a different hand at a later date and partitioned into three rooms over which some bedrooms had been added. 'Inconvenience and dilapidation were the keynotes of the house when the Duke and Duchess first visited it in 1931', Sir John Wheeler-Bennett writes. Yet so beautiful is the situation and so beautiful, surely, were the sad remains, it is no wonder the royal couple quickly fell in love with it. 1931, after the crash of the New York stock exchange and the subsequent world depression, was scarcely propitious to the rebuilding of the house – and indeed in this year the Duke sold his horses and gave up hunting – but, as the economic crisis passed, the partitions were removed from the great saloon and new pink-washed wings were added to provide a delightful and suitable royal home.

Queen Mary was a passionate gardener and both her sons had inherited this taste. Like the Prince of Wales at Fort Belvedere, the Duke of York enjoyed all the aspects of gardening, not merely the landscaping and planning (and here he was lucky in the presence of Mr Eric Savill, who created the Savill Garden in Windsor Park) but the hard slog and the skilled job (it is said that he had 'green fingers'). His speciality was shrubs and among these the rhododendron. He once wrote a bread and butter letter expressing his thoughts in the names of rhododendron plants. Thus of his wife who had been absent through illness, 'I found her looking Microlecucrem' (small and white).

All these pleasures the Duchess shared, as she shared the burdens of his public life and his devotion to this children.

FOUR

THE ABDICATION

IN JANUARY 1936 King George V died and his eldest son succeeded him. As King Edward VIII was not married, the Duke of York then became Heir Apparent. Before the year was out, Edward VIII had abdicated and his brother succeeded him.

The strangest thing about the strange affair of the Abdication is that, with the exception of King George V, no one seemed to have expected it. Edward VIII was forty-two when he abdicated, but none of the younger members of his family and not one of his closest friends seem ever to have recognised the strength of the egotism which made him capable of such an irrational and reckless act. It may be too much to suggest that his father actually envisaged the act of abdication but two remarks he made, although recorded in the aftermath of history, seem too specific to have been embellished or misremembered and show that he was aware that his son had a pathological unbalance which might lead him to some act of the kind. He said to Baldwin: 'After I am dead the boy will ruin himself in twelve months,' and he is quoted by Lady Airlie as saying: 'I pray to God that my eldest son will never marry and have children, and that nothing will come between Bertie and Lilibet and the throne.'

The wildness and anxiety of these two remarks make it even stranger that, when the Abdication finally came, it took everyone by surprise. When nearly forty years later someone remarked to Mrs Dudley Ward: 'He must have been a very peculiar man,' she replied quite simply, 'I didn't think so.' Someone else who knew him very well, on being asked whether she had felt the magnetic charm attributed to the Prince, replied: 'I didn't think of him like that. I thought him rather pathetic.' But she denied that she had noticed any quality by which one might have predicted his act. His brothers, too, seem to have been totally unprepared, while, when his purpose became obvious, his mother thought his mind temporarily unhinged. Consequently, when the Yorks heard, as everyone else in a small circle in London heard, rumours that he intended to marry Mrs Simpson, they did not believe them. There are certain acts – murder is an obvious if extreme example – which, in connection with anyone one knows well, are outside the bounds of possibility. To members of the Royal Family, the act of renouncing the Crown is one.

During the whole of the Abdication crisis Edward VIII behaved to his family, lovers and friends with a cold and childish lack of feeling reminiscent of an Evelyn Waugh heroine, Brenda Last or Lady Metroland. For weeks at a time he did not communicate with his mother, he was unavailable to his brothers and he allowed his family to learn, as everyone else did, his intentions from the Press. The Duke of York, if he abdicated, would inherit the Crown, but he neither consulted him nor took him into his confidence, merely allowing him to await an increasingly inevitable outcome. The Abdication took place on 11 December 1936. In the first week of November the Duke of York wrote to Queen Mary:

'I have been meaning to come & see you but I wanted to see David first. He is very difficult to see & when one does he wants to talk about other matters.

'It is all so worrying & I feel we all live a life of conjecture; never knowing what will happen tomorrow, & then the unexpected comes. . . .'

On 29 November the Duke wrote to Sir Eric Miéville:

'I hate going to Scotland to do what I have to do as I am so worried over this whole matter. I feel like the proverbial "sheep being led to the slaughter".'

And most revealing of all, are the December entries in his diary:

'I returned to London from Edinburgh on the morning of Thursday December 3rd. At Euston I was both surprised and horrified to see that the posters of the Daily Press had the following as their headlines in block letters "The King's Marriage". . . . On my return I hastened to see Queen Mary & to tell her how surprised I was that the whole matter had been published. I saw my brother . . . who was in a great stage of excitement, who said he would leave the country as King after making a broadcast to his subjects & leave it to them to decide what should be done. The Prime Minister went to see him at 9.0 PM that evening & later (in Mary's and my presence) David said to Queen Mary that he could not live alone as King and must marry Mrs ——. When David left after making this dreadful announcement to his mother he told me to come and see him at the Fort next morning. I rang him up but he would not see me and put me off till Saturday. I told him I would be at Royal Lodge on Saturday by 12.30 PM. I rang him up Saturday. "Come & see me on Sunday" was his answer. "I will see you & tell you my decision when I have made up my mind." Sunday evening I rang up. "The King has a conference & will speak to you later" was the answer. But he did not ring me up. Monday morning came. I rang up at 1.0 PM & my brother told me he might be able to see me that evening. I told him "I must go to London but would come to the Fort when he wanted me". I did not go to London but waited. I sent a telephone message to the Fort to say that if I was wanted I would be at Royal Lodge. My brother rang me up at 10 minutes to 7.0 PM to say "Come & see me after dinner". I said "No, I will come & see you at once". I was with him at 7.0 PM. The awful & ghastly suspense of waiting was over. I found him pacing up & down the room, & he told me his decision that he would go. I went back to Royal Lodge for dinner & returned to the Fort later. I felt having once got there I was not going to leave. As he is my eldest brother I had to be there to try & help him in his hour of need.

'I went back to London that night with my wife.'

On Saturday afternoon, 5 December, Walter Monckton acting for the King formally told the Prime Minister, Stanley Baldwin, of the King's decision to abdicate. Baffy Dugdale writing in her diary the following Monday records:

'The King's *one* idea is Mrs Simpson. Nothing that stands between him and her will meet his approval. The Crown is only valuable if it would interest *her*. He must have marriage because then she can be with him always. Therefore he has no wish to form a "Party" who would keep him on the throne and let her be his mistress. Therefore he has no animosity against Ministers who are not opposing his abdication.... I do not think, in the light of this knowledge, that there is much danger of a King's Party. It is impossible to be *"plus royaliste que le roi".'*

On Tuesday 8 December Baldwin went to Fort Belvedere in a last, unsuccessful attempt to persuade the King to give up Mrs Simpson and remain on the throne. That night nine men dined at Fort Belvedere – the King, the Dukes of York and Kent, Walter Monckton and Mr Baldwin among them. The King had appeared to be in the last stages of nervous exhaustion and Monckton had persuaded him to dine in his bedroom alone. The rest of the company had therefore actually sat down to dinner when he came in dressed in his white kilt and, in Monckton's words 'with his boyish face and smile, with a good fresh colour while the rest of us were as pale as sheets, rippling over with bright conversation, and with a careful eye to see that his guests were being looked after'. The generous and modest Duke of York wrote:

'My brother was the life and soul of the party, telling the PM things I am sure he had never heard before about unemployed centres, etc (referring to his visit to S. Wales). I whispered to W.M. "& this is the man we are going to lose". One couldn't, nobody could, believe it.'

The following morning, in reply to a formal message from the Cabinet expressing the hope that His Majesty would 'reconsider an intention which must so deeply distress and so vitally affect all Your Majesty's subjects', the King replied:

'His Majesty has given the matter his further consideration but regrets he is unable to alter his decision.'

Nothing but the formalities remained.

On 9 December the Duke of York received Walter Monckton and Sir Edward Peacock (acting as the King's financial adviser) 'where they reported to him and secured his assent to His Majesty retaining Royal Rank & that if and when he is allowed to come to England he should have the Fort to live in'. After this he went again to the Fort where he had a long talk with his brother, 'but I could see that nothing I said would alter his decision'. Later in the day he went back to London and went to see Queen Mary.

'When I told her what had happened, I broke down and sobbed like a child,' he wrote in his diary, while Queen Mary recorded in hers:

'Bertie arrived very late from Fort Belvedere and Mr Walter Monckton brought him and me the paper drawn up for David's abdication of the throne of this Empire because he wants to marry Mrs Simpson!!!!! The whole affair has lasted since 16 November and is very painful. It is a terrible blow to us all and particularly to poor Bertie.'

The following day, 10 December, the Duke of York went once more to Fort Belvedere where he and his younger brothers witnessed the King sign the instrument of Abdication. 'Perfectly calm D signed 5 or 6 copies of the instrument and then 5 copies of his message to Parliament, one for each Dominion Parliament. It was a dreadful moment & one never to be forgotten by those present.'

On that day, too, at a meeting which the Duke of York described as 'a dreadful lawyer/interview', a general settlement was reached about the financial arrangements for the abdicating King.

Under the wills of Queen Victoria and King George v, Edward viii was a life tenant of both Sandringham and Balmoral, although these were clearly his because of the natural assumption that during his lifetime he would be King. Nevertheless, any financial arrangement satisfactory to all had to be based on a transfer of both estates to his brother. King Edward viii cared nothing either for Sandringham or for Balmoral, which were to him merely places where his father had lived and where he had usually been bored or ill at ease. All his heart was given to Fort Belvedere, which he loved, as he loved Mrs Simpson, exclusively. When he succeeded to the throne he had made economies at both the royal estates (economies which were in themselves necessary) caring nothing for the welfare of men who had served his father for years. King George vi carried on all the necessary economies but every man was looked after and none left except with a pension or to another job. The terms of the final arrangement between the two brothers have never been made public but it is generally believed that the Duke of Windsor received a very large capital sum.

Late on the night of 10 December the Duke of York motored back to London and to his home in Piccadilly. When he approached his house he found a large crowd outside it cheering madly. 'I was overwhelmed,' he wrote.

The Coronation of King George VI.

The King presents a cup to the Boys' Boxing
Champion of 1938.

King George and Queen Elizabeth with Monsieur Lebrun, the President of France,
at a garden party near Paris in 1938.

Overleaf The King and Queen and the two Princesses talking to guests and members of the
Company of Archers during the 'Reddendo' ceremony at Holyrood Palace in 1937.

Above A picnic at Balmoral in 1938.

Opposite above The King and his daughters about to set out for a ride at Windsor on Princess Elizabeth's thirteenth birthday.

Opposite below Royal Lodge Windsor.

Queen Mary greeting her daughter-in-law in 1937.

All through the last weeks of the Abdication the Duchess of York had been ill with flu, and the Duke of York had travelled down to Windsor every day, and back to London in the evening. On this night in December, when returned to his house through the cheering crowds, although she was not yet fully recovered, she was waiting up to welcome him. Both now knew he would inherit the throne, and she accepted her fate with the unemphatic courage which was to be the inspiration of those who worked for her for the rest of her life.

One further event concerning the ex-King must be recorded. When Walter Monckton went to the Chateau de Candé near Tours to attend the wedding of the Duke and Duchess of Windsor, he carried with him messages of goodwill from his brother but a letter in which King George wrote that he had been pleased by Letters Patent 'to declare that the Duke of Windsor shall, notwithstanding his act of Abdication ... be entitled to hold and enjoy for himself only the style and attribute of Royal Highness, so however that his wife and descendants, if any, shall not hold she said title or attribute'. The Duke of Windsor was to be HRH: his wife was not.

The Duke of Windsor never forgave and never recovered from what he was bound to regard as a totally unnecessary and completely unexpected insult to his wife. It is not true to say, as has been said, that this caused a breach between himself and his family, because, in spite of it, he never ceased untiring efforts to persuade them to receive his wife. So that, although it is true that he savagely resented both that the title was withheld from her and that she was never welcomed by his family, the breach between him and them was caused by the Abdication and not by any subsequent event. But the exclusion of the Duchess from a title which most people had assumed would be hers automatically, hurt him desperately, hit her very hard and has been criticised by many people. Most of these criticisms were on humanitarian grounds and were best expressed by Walter Monckton in a diary written at the time.

'When he (the Duke of Windsor) had been King', Monckton wrote, 'he was told he could not marry Mrs Simpson because she would have to take his status and become Queen, so he gave up his Kingdom and Empire to make her his wife. He could not give up his royal birth, or his right to be called "His Royal Highness" which flowed from it. It was a little hard to be told, when he did marry her, that she would not have the same status as himself.'

Recent publications have made it clear that, once it was put to the Government and the Dominions that Letters Patent should be issued which, while confirming the ex-King his royal rank, should specifically exclude his wife and any descendants, agreement was virtually unanimous (on being told that on her marriage Mrs Simpson would be known as 'Her Grace the Duchess of Windsor' Mr Savage of New Zealand replied: 'And quite enough too.'). Yet there is little doubt that the suggestion came in the first place from King George himself, who made it with the full support of his wife and mother. The Royal Family were still in a state of shock as a result of the Abdication and the particular circumstances which had brought it about. They had (wrongly as it turned out) little faith in the durability of a marriage between a man they believed to be obsessed and deranged and a women whose third living husband he proposed to become. ('His family were wondering what will become of him,' Baldwin said to his niece, 'when he discovers what sort she really is.') It was the possibility that the marriage would not last that caused the King's fears. 'Once a person has become a Royal Highness,' he reminded Baldwin, 'there is no means of depriving her of the title.' Nor can it be thought highly imaginative in the circumstances to visualise the possibility of a series of degradations to the monarchical principle over which the court and the sovereign would have no control.

One thing that must strike the student of the Abdication crisis and its aftermath is that the nearer one gets to the centre the more painfully it will be found to have been felt. To the people of Great Britain and the Commonwealth it was little more than a nine days wonder, their feeling for the Crown being too strong to be broken by one aberrant act. However, those who had had closer relations with the ex-King – regimental officers, social workers and so on – felt more personally let down, while the Prime Minister and the King's Household were not merely over-fearful of the damage to the Crown but often outraged. Most ashamed, humiliated and angry of all, were the ex-King's family to whom his act was incomprehensible as well as unforgivable. Queen Mary felt acutely that the concept for which men had been asked to die in 1914 was 'Your King and Country', and she referred to this in a letter to the Duke of Windsor the following year.

> 'I do not think', she wrote, 'you have ever realized the shock which the attitude you took caused your family and the whole Nation. It seemed inconceivable to those who made such sacrifices during the war that you, as their King, refused a lesser sacrifice.'

And she added:

> 'All my life I have put my Country before everything else, and I simply cannot change now.'

The last sentence may be taken absolutely literally. The enormous growth in popularity of King George v and Queen Mary and, in consequence, of the Monarchy as an institution owed more than anything to the fact that all their lives they put their country before anything else. That the new King shared his mother's feelings, both of shame and of the duty of the Royal Family, is made clear in this sentence from a letter he wrote Mr Baldwin at the time. 'I hope', he said, 'that time will be allowed to me to make amends for what has happened.'

The key to the dedication of the Royal Family lies in the Coronation service. One month before the Duke of Windsor's marriage, George VI was crowned at the service which had originally been intended for his brother. The Coronation is essentially a religious ceremony.

'It is the Archbishop who presents the King to the people for their acclamation; it is he who anoints the King, who hands the Sword to him, who delivers the Orb with the cross shining upon it, who places in his hand the Sceptre and receiving the Crown from the Altar sets it on the King's head. All through the service the Archbishop blessing and exhorting the King is also hallowing the State. And throughout the rite the King is seeking the help of God for his great office, now kneeling previous to the anointing while the Holy Spirit is invoked, afterwards for the Archbishop's blessing, later to make his oblation, and finally to receive Holy Communion.'

Psychologists have paid some attention to the emotions of society as a whole at the time of a Coronation, to the sense of 'inspiration' and 're-dedication of the nation' which seems to be commonly experienced and they have pointed out that acts of communion are communal acts, between the deity or those who are the symbols of the highest values of the community, and persons who come together to be in communion with one another through their common contact with the sacred. No attempt has ever been made, nor since it has so limited an application, is ever likely to be made to understand the effect of the Coronation ceremony on the person or persons who represent the symbols of the highest values of the community. Yet it requires no great feat of imagination to appreciate the magnitude of the emotional stamina required to accept the symbolic role at the time of the ceremony and for the rest of a lifetime. At the moment of the anointment both King George VI and Queen Elizabeth experienced a spiritual transformation of a metaphysical kind, through which their already strong sense of duty was transmuted to dedication of a specifically religious character. Many interpretations might be put upon this, what remains indisputable is the fact, without recognition of which no one can understand the course of their lives.

It is therefore a trivial and ignorant view of the exaltation and isolation demanded of them, to expect that in the interests of a flabby kind of live-and-let-live philosophy they should also be willing to bestow the symbols of their rank on a woman who fulfilled none of the requirements of it, and who, they were surely justified, if arguably incorrect, in believing had obsessed and deranged the mind of the man who should have been the first to uphold it.

Doubts have been expressed as to the legality of the Act which deprived the Duchess of the title HRH. In fact the question of legality seems not to arise, since this was not a matter for Parliament – as it would have been had it concerned a member of Parliament – but of the Royal Prerogative, that is to say a matter on which the King alone could decide by reason of his sovereign position under the constitution. The question therefore is one of logic and justice.

King George VI based his view of the case on the Letters Patent which defined and limited those who 'should have and at all times hold and enjoy' the title Royal Highness to the children of any sovereign, the children of the sons of any such Sovereign and the eldest living son of the eldest son of the Prince of Wales. In the Letters Patents which regulated the titles of the Duke and Duchess of Windsor it is taken for granted that the whole purpose of the former Letters Patent was to restrict the title of Royal Highness to those in direct line to the throne, and it is difficult to see what other meaning they could have. Yet if the lineal argument is accepted, it will be found to stand the logic of Walter Monckton's view (see p. 61) on its head. If Mrs Simpson was not suited to be Queen then for exactly the same reasons she was not suited to hold a title restricted to those in line for the throne. Nor does it need emphasis that this was not a view which could be held for a period of time and then abandoned in the interests of a policy of 'forgive and forget'.

One point which gives strength to the arguments of those who believe that the Duchess of Windsor was 'deprived' of her natural rights is that when the Duke of York married Lady Elizabeth Bowes-Lyon, it was announced that his wife would take 'the title, style or attribute of Royal Highness in accordance with the settled general rule that a wife takes the status of her husband'. One cannot dispute the meaning of that, but it must be remembered that the unwritten law thus acknowledged was expected to apply only to marriages already approved by the King. As with all the other circumstances surrounding the Abdication, there was no precedent for the marriage of an ex-King. Yet no one can seriously doubt that from Queen Victoria onwards every Sovereign of Great Britain, Ireland, and the British Dominions beyond the Seas, King Emperor of India, would have agreed with King George VI's interpretation of the Letters Patent regulating the rank of Royal Highness and to the need to exclude Mrs Simpson from it.

FIVE

KING AND QUEEN: AT WAR

KING GEORGE VI and Queen Elizabeth restored the stability of the Crown after the Abdication crisis not by what they did but by what they were. Walter Monckton has quoted Edward VIII as saying that, if the people were wanting someone exactly reproducing his father, there was the Duke of York. One cannot escape the note of weariness, even contempt in this statement, but the truth is that the British people did desire their King to have all the more important qualities of George V. At the time of the old King's Jubilee, everyone, including himself, was taken by surprise by the warmth of feeling the crowds exhibited. What they liked about him was not his charm, for he had very little, but his goodness: his devotion to themselves and the country and his reputation for straightforwardness in all his dealings. King George VI had inherited all his father's best qualities and, although neither had great originality or intellect, they were more than merely men of good character. Possibly as a result of their upbringing and training, they were both men of high purpose, of noble dedication, and, if not selfless in all things, certainly unwavering in their pursuit of duty.

One need not be a psychologist to know that, if the Crown is to survive, it must be immaculate. When the British at last understood the reasons which prompted Edward VIII to renounce the throne, love died over night; and because the Press had preserved complete silence on the rumours that he intended to marry Mrs Simpson until the end, the Abdication came more as a sudden blow than as a long debilitating illness. As with other superficial wounds, recovery was swift.

Indeed, in the higher ranks of society and among those who had sought the friendship of Edward VIII and Mrs Simpson, the speed and thoroughness with which the late King was denied and the new one appeased was regarded as, to say the least of it, inelegant. Yet, even in the hysteria and panic caused by personal ambition there was present an emotion which swept the whole country and seemed wholly admirable where there was no element of self-seeking. All ranks of the British people had received a shock, since even those who knew him well had not believed that in the last resort the King would abdicate the Crown rather than give up Mrs

Simpson. All rallied to the new King and Queen as a return to safety and once more Harold Nicolson voices the opinion of the day in the following passage:

> 'The Queen then goes the rounds. She wears upon her face a faint smile indicative of how much she would liked her dinner party were it not for the fact that she was Queen of England. Nothing could exceed the charm or dignity which she displays and I cannot help feeling what a mess poor Mrs Simpson would have made of such an occasion.'

And if the new King had not the exceptional public personality of his brother, he inspired confidence and, as the latter was prone to remark when at the end he wished to press his brother's claims: 'He has one matchless blessing enjoyed by so many of you and not by me – a happy home with his wife and children.'

It is generally accepted that the concept of the family plays a large part in the attachment of the British to the monarchy. 'The monarchy is idealised not so much for the virtue of the individual sovereign as for the virtue he expresses in his family life.' All the interest the Australians had shown in the baby Princess Elizabeth was felt at least equally in Great Britain, while the appearance of the two unexpectedly pretty little girls, when they were old enough to be photographed, was clearly a tremendous bonus. (Unexpected because the odds against such good looks in a single family which inherits the Crown must be high.)

The new King took easily to his role. Even in the first days, with all the haggling about Sandringham and Balmoral and the question of what the ex-King should be called, he was both authoritative and regal. Once more his performance is quite different from the impression of his personality given by historians. In 1974, when the Duke of Windsor died, it was possible for a playwright, who had clearly done considerable research into his subject, to present George VI on the stage at the time of the Abdication as not merely practically unable to speak but completely distraught. The job of a writer is a difficult one because history is distorted by chance remarks which after much repetition become part of the canon. Even biographers most sympathetic to George VI are inclined to conjecture that the Queen married him because she saw in him qualities which were fully developed only later in life. And here is Harold Nicolson's account written after an interview with Queen Mary. She said ... that 'the present King had been appalled when he succeeded. He was devoted to his brother, and the whole Abdication crisis made him miserable. He sobbed on my shoulder for a whole hour – there, upon that sofa.'

Even the shortest reflection would convince one that this remark, if it was ever made, was a figure of speech. In the first place it is physically impossible to sob for a whole hour; in the second, inconceivable that the King, had he felt constrained to do so, should choose Queen Mary's shoulder to lie upon – not merely because he had plenty of experience of its severity, but because the Queen surely would not have welcomed so extreme a display of distaste for the Crown and for what, however unwillingly he accepted it, was now her son's duty. Yet it is the kind of thing that gives the impression that at this time of life the King was unable to sustain the role and only grew into manhood with the help of his wife.

That he was entirely dependent on Queen Elizabeth no one who saw them could doubt. But there was a duality here which has been already described and what he willingly asked she willingly gave. To depend on someone who loves you is not necessarily a sign of weakness – it may even be the reverse.

Luckily the King kept a diary, because there is no doubt he speaks best for himself. (This has already been noted in relation to his letters to his father during his service in the Navy, his account of Jutland and so on.) He was an extremely religious man and, as has already been said, his Coronation was a spiritual experience which altered his whole life. 'I am quite sure', the Bishop of St Albans wrote to the Queen, 'that those whose privilege it was to be near Your Majesties must have felt – as I did – that this sense of reality was mainly due to the lovely way ... in which Your Majesties, together, made us all realize that Your Coronation meant for You, both first and foremost, the Offering of Yourselves and all You had to give in life-long service to God & Your fellow men, in simple faith that he would give You the power equal to the task.'

Yet here is part of the King's own account of the ceremony, which, while it shows his meticulous attention to detail, as an example of understatement can hardly be beaten.

'After the Introduction I removed my Parliamentary Robes & Cap of Maintenance & moved to the Coronation Chair. Here various vestments were placed upon me, the white Colobium Sindonis, a surplice which the Dean of Westminster insisted I should put on inside out, had not my Groom of the Robes come to the rescue. Before this I knelt at the Altar to take the Coronation Oath. I had two Bishops, Durham & Bath & Wells, one on either side to support me & hold the form of Service for me to follow. When this great moment came neither Bishop could find the words, so the Archbishop held his book down for me to read, but horror of horrors, his thumb covered the words of the Oath.

'My Lord Great Chamberlain was supposed to dress me but I found his hands fumbled and shook so I had to fix the belt of the sword myself. As it was he nearly put the hilt of the sword under my chin trying to attach it to the belt. At last all the various vestments were put on & the Archbishop had given me the two sceptres. I had taken every precaution as I thought to see that the Crown was put on the right way round, but the Dean & the Archbishop had been juggling with it so much that I never did know whether it was right or not. The St Edward's Crown, the Crown of England, weighs 7 lbs & it had to fit. Then I rose to my feet & walked to the throne in the centre of the amphitheatre. As I turned after leaving the Coronation Chair I was brought up all standing, owing to one of the Bishops treading on my robe. I had to tell him to get off it pretty sharply as I nearly fell down.'

It seems clear here, as often elsewhere, that the King is keeping his diary for posterity. It is not mere jottings, and the explanation of the weight of St Edward's Crown, for instance, is written as though for the better understanding of someone else.

The King, like his father and grandfather, had an ungovernable temper, although, like his father and grandfather, he was always ready to apologise for it. But, as one of the Royal Household was to say many years later: 'When the King loses his temper everyone scuttles. There is less incentive to control it when it clearly pays to lose it.'

The one thing that George VI had seriously to struggle against for the whole of his life was his stammer. Where his other difficulties seem to be magnified, this is sometimes minimised, possibly because in his lifetime everyone wished to encourage him. He learned to control it but only through the care with which he prepared public speeches. These were rehearsed again and again with Logue in attendance to give advice as to breathing. Here is an account of the preparations for one of his first major appearances as King. The speech from the throne at the opening of Parliament is delivered sitting which greatly increases the difficulty for someone who stammers because the sitting position inhibits the rhythm of breathing, an intrinsic part of the method the King had been taught. 'Sitting in his study at Buckingham Palace, with the Crown upon his head, King George VI practised indefatigably, first with the text of his father's last Speech from the Throne in 1935, and then with the draft of his own. His efforts were rewarded with a success which, if tempered by some hesitation, was considerably greater than he had ever expected.'

There are also several accounts of the King's speeches written by those who listened to him. This is the record of a luncheon, arranged by the Empire Parliamentary Association in honour of the Dominion Prime Ministers, in the first year of the King's reign written by Chips Channon.

'Soon Trumpeters in new liveries blew on silver bugles to announce the arrival of the King. He walked alone, a trifle awkwardly but not without charm and we watched the dignitaries being presented to him ... Then luncheon ... Then Hailsham stood, proposed His Majesty's Health, and the King rose, the amplifier was put in front of him, and for a few terrible seconds there was dead silence, as he could not (that is his trouble and failing) get the words out. A feeling of uneasiness came over the crowd; but soon the King, controlling himself, read out a short speech of thanks. As he went on he seemed to warm up, and finished in good style, and sat down amidst great applause and relief.

'This evening I thought of the grave, grey Speaker of the House of Commons and his dignified address to the assembled delegates, and the King, faltering, with

1940 – the King and Queen talking to workmen who were demolishing bomb-damaged buildings in London.

The King visits the Generals: (*left*) with General Mark Clark at the North African Front in 1943; (*above*) with General Alexander during a visit to the Polish troops fighting with the Eighth Army in Italy in 1944; and (*below*) with General Montgomery who is introducing his driver to the King.

Above While visiting the Scots Guards in August 1940, the King sent for Mr William Fellowes (now Sir William) his agent at Sandringham. The expression on the King's face is caused by the sight of Mr Fellowes's regulation battle dress which had not yet been fitted.

Above right The King visits the troops: sighting a bren during a practise low-bombing attack with the Welsh Guards.

Right The King talks to a fighter-pilot during a visit to a station of the RAF fighter command.

Overleaf Buckingham Palace is bombed.

Left Although being hurried to an air-raid shelter during a visit to bomb sites, the Queen cannot resist a cat.

Opposite above The King surrounded by smiling faces on a visit to the East End of London during the Blitz.

Opposite below The Royal car passing through the streets of Valetta during the King's visit to Malta to present the island with the George Cross.

Below The King and Queen visiting a munitions factory in 1942.

Left Sandringham Park was ploughed-up during the war and used for cultivation. The King was very particular over the use of petrol and is seen here with his family and Charley French, a groom retired from a life in the Royal Mews, visiting the estate by pony-trap and bicycle during the harvest of 1943.

Above The Queen with the two Princesses who are in Pantomime costume for a Christmas entertainment in 1941 at Sandringham.

Overleaf VE Day.

his halting speech and resigned kindly smile, and everyone pretending that he had done it well.'

While as late as 1945, when the King had gained enormously in confidence, Harold Nicolson writes of a ceremony in the Royal Gallery as follows:

'The King read a long speech. He has a really beautiful voice and it is to be regretted that his stammer makes it almost intolerably painful to listen to him. It is as if one read a fine piece of prose written on a typewriter the keys of which stick from time to time and mar the beauty of the whole. It makes him stress the wrong word. "My Lords and Members ... of the House of Commons."'

It seems reasonable therefore to believe that it was his stammer which encouraged a nervousness in disposition rather than the other way round. It takes enormous courage to speak on major occasions in public with the knowledge that only complete control can avoid disaster.

In any case, the King quickly grew to his role. Eye-witnesses are soon remarking on his popularity, on his increased presence and dignity and, most telling of all, on his remarkable likeness to Edward VIII. The Queen predictably captured everyone.

●

All this was well because the King had inherited the long, slow decline of England's power and prestige which ended in the Second World War. In the spring of 1936, while his brother still reigned, German troops had entered the Rhineland bringing to an end the hopes of those who believed in collective security. That year saw the Rome–Berlin Axis agreements and during the period while the British Government were forced to attend to the crisis of the Abdication (in October 1936 the Prime Minister, Stanley Baldwin, asked the Foreign Secretary, Anthony Eden to 'try not to bother me too much with foreign affairs just now'), Germany signed the anti-Comintern pact with Japan and Fascist soldiers entered Spain.

Immediately after the King's Coronation Ramsay MacDonald resigned as Lord President of the Council and Stanley Baldwin as Prime Minister, bringing to an end the régime which had lasted since 1931. Faced with the undisguised and un-challenged aggression of the Axis Powers, Neville Chamberlain, who succeeded as Prime Minister, was forced to choose between an attempt to form an alliance of anti-Axis Powers, or an attempt to appease Germany. The events which followed his choice of the latter course are too well known to require elaboration here except in so far as the King played a part in them.

Like his elder brother, George VI had a horror of war based on the actual experience of it. Apart from his naval service he had visited the Prince of Wales in France and had seen both British and German bombardments and the shelling of villages by the Germans. Later generations have proved particularly sensitive to the horror of the 1914 war but possibly have less understanding of those who, having lived through it, succeeded to a world where there were two million women whose natural mates had been killed, where the consequent depression left as many unemployed and where almost every family remembered someone killed. The King was not alone in being emotionally unable to confront the need for another war, and, since his fears were for his countrymen, rather than himself, there was nothing ignoble in his eagerness to believe it might be avoided. In addition he liked and trusted Neville Chamberlain, and so, when the latter set out on the long humiliating series of visits and negotiations with Hitler, he did so with the King's backing. When Anthony Eden resigned rather than be a party to re-opening negotiations with Italy in an attempt to divide the Axis Powers, although the King much regretted his departure, he was personally more at ease with his successor, Lord Halifax.

George VI was tremendously eager to serve. All through September 1938, when Chamberlain travelled backwards and forwards to Germany in an effort which finally averted war for the period of one year, the King was anxious to make a personal appeal to Hitler, on the basis of 'one ex-Serviceman to another', and in 1939 he suggested using his cousin Prince Philip of Hesse as 'a messenger to convey to Hitler that we are really in earnest'. In 1939 his Private Secretary, Sir Alexander Hardinge, wrote to the Permanent Under-Secretary for Foreign Affairs, saying that the King had closely watched the effect of the German–Soviet Pact on Japan and would be disappointed if no benefit was derived from it. 'His Majesty wonders, therefore, if it would help in any way if, at an opportune moment, he were to send a friendly message direct to the Emperor.' In August 1939 the King wished to follow the lead of King Leopold of the Belgians, President Roosevelt and Pope Pius XII in making a direct appeal to Hitler.

None of these offers were approved. Power had changed hands since the time when nearly every ruler in Europe was a relation of the British Royal Family, while the complexity of the issues was so great and their outcome so uncertain that the prestige of the King had to be protected against rebuff. In any case it is doubtful whether these interventions from one crowned head to another ever had much effect. The power of the modern monarch lies, as in reality it did with Edward VII, in the un-defined and probably indefinable appeal that royalty has to mankind. The institution is symbolic and the King stands for all the virtues, heroic as well as domestic, and is supported by magnificent traditional ceremonial. The elected heads of state are no less susceptible to all this than their predecessors and when the character and personality of the Sovereign is sufficient to sustain the role, as it has been in Great Britain for more than a hundred years, the prestige of the country is enormously upheld. Looking back, it must be regarded as very fortunate that it fell to George VI and not to his wilful and impatient brother to learn the limitations and opportunities of the twentieth-century monarchy.

The King found his feet not in Great Britain but on a visit to Canada and the United States of America in 1939. In the summer of 1937 Mr Mackenzie King had proposed a royal visit to Canada, and hearing of this President Roosevelt had instructed his special envoy to suggest that he might visit Washington as well. The President then followed this instruction with a personal invitation, the first direct correspondence to be exchanged between a President of the United States and a British Sovereign.

> 'Frankly I think it would be an excellent thing for Anglo-American relations if you could visit the United States … if you bring either or both of the children with you they will also be very welcome, and I shall try to have one or two Roosevelts of approximately the same age to play with them!'

The final arrangements for the visit were delayed because of the crisis in European affairs but on 5 May 1939 the King and Queen sailed from Southampton in the liner *Empress Australia*, which for the purposes of the voyage was rated as a 'Royal Yacht', and which was accompanied half-way across the Atlantic by the battle-cruiser *Repulse*.

It is common when attempting to analyse the appeal of the Royal Family to speak of the emotions of the 'British People', but this is because the British are among the few nations still to have a constitutional monarchy. The sense of the mystery and magic, the identification with symbols of virtue, the desire to pay homage, the hundred-and-one unanalysable strands of emotion which make up the British attachment to the Crown are felt all over the world. The present Queen's visit to the United States of America in 1976 was but the latest proof that, while British prestige diminishes, the prestige of the Crown does not. In 1939, when for the first time the Canadians were able to welcome their Sovereign in person and when for the first time he presided in person over the Parliament at Ottawa, they were swept away by the emotions of loyalty and devotion which were to carry them into the Second World War as it had into the First. 'It was wonderful', Lord Tweedsmuir wrote, 'to see old fellows weeping and crying "Ay man, if Hitler could just see this."'

Everywhere they went the King and Queen spoke to the people personally, always asking to be allowed to get nearer the crowds. 'Our Monarchs are most remarkable young people,' Lord Tweedsmuir wrote in the same letter. 'The King is a wonderful mixture of shrewdness, kindliness and humour. As for the Queen she has a perfect genius for the right kind of publicity.'

When on 9 June the King and Queen reached America it was once more the first visit of a reigning British Sovereign.

'My husband invited them to Washington', Mrs Roosevelt wrote later, 'largely because, believing that we all might soon be engaged in a life and death struggle, in which Great Britain would be our first line of defence, he hoped that the visit would create a bond of friendship between the people of the two countries.' And she added, 'In many ways it proved even more successful than he had expected.'

In New York City the King and Queen were received by enormous crowds, cheering and singing 'Rule Britannia', while on the ninety-mile drive from there to

President Roosevelt's home at Hyde Park they were met in every small town by masses of people, the ringing of church bells and flower-strewn roads.

It had been decided that the King should not be accompanied by Lord Halifax, the Foreign Secretary, so that the visit could not be considered to have political implications, but he had two conversations with Roosevelt, the first accompanied by the Canadian Prime Minister, Mr Mackenzie King, the second alone. He returned to London with notes of these conversations which in the event showed Roosevelt to have been in too optimistic a mood, since he believed that, if London were bombed, it would bring the United States into the war, but which also foreshadowed the Lease-Lend Agreement of 1941.

The effect of this visit was threefold. First it was of undoubted if incalculable benefit to Anglo-American relations at that time. Second, of perhaps more lasting importance, a genuine friendship had been made between the King and Queen and the President. It is well known that the President carried on a correspondence with Winston Churchill throughout the war years as between two 'naval persons', which greatly increased the opportunity and speed of exchange of ideas. What is not so widely known is that he also corresponded with the King.

Thirdly, it is once more true to say that the effect of these visits on the King and Queen themselves was as important as the impression they made on others. The King came back with faith in himself.

✒

The Reign of George VI will be chiefly remembered for the manner of its beginning and for the Second World War. During the five years of war the King's mood was always in tune with his people's. Thus, although he had approved of the policy of appeasement and had taken time to convince himself of the necessity to fight, his mood changed as quickly and as completely as theirs did. The one certain gain from Munich was that it gave the British time to adjust to their fate, and their confidence and pugnacity in war, following the long years of vacillation which preceded it, took even themselves by surprise.

'The capacity of the British people for illogical virtue in politics is equalled only by their absolute refusal to recognise defeat and their ability to deck their disasters with the laurels of victory,' George VI's biographer wrote. And: 'Personally I feel happier now that we have no allies to be polite to and pamper,' the King wrote to his mother after the fall of France.

The courage of the British in the Second World War owed more to the leaders they threw up at the time than to anything else. It is the fashion for military historians to criticise Winston Churchill's conduct of the war. Yet no one who lived through it ever doubts that, without him, it might have been lost in the first year. It was the spirit of the British that carried them through while they stood alone. This spirit was aroused by Winston Churchill but it was sustained and very much nourished by the King and Queen, and this, as with Winston Churchill, was a result of their courage as well as of their position. Both the King and Queen had instruction in firing a revolver. 'I shall not go down like the others,' the Queen said.

Throughout the whole course of the war, the King's visits to his troops on every front and the constant presence of the King and Queen on the bomb sites, where people stood by the shattered ruins of their homes, brought comfort and courage to others.

'I dined with Billy Harlech last night [Harold Nicolson wrote] the Regional Commissioner. He had been spending the day with the Queen visiting Sheffield. He says that when the car stops, the Queen nips out into the snow and goes straight into the middle of the crowd and starts talking to them. For a moment or two they just gaze and gape in astonishment. But then they all start talking at once. "Hi! Your Majesty! Look here!" She has that quality of making everybody feel that they and they alone are being spoken to. It is, I think, because she has very large eyes which she opens very wide and turns straight upon one. Billy Harlech says these visits do incalculable good.'

'Your Majesties are more beloved by all classes and conditions,' Winston Churchill wrote to the King, 'than any of the princes of the past.'

And it seems likely that it was more because of the quality of genuine sincerity in the King and Queen's devotion to their people than because she opened her eyes very wide that they were so much beloved.

'I feel quite exhausted after seeing and hearing so much sadness, sorrow, heroism and magnificent spirit,' Queen Elizabeth wrote to Queen Mary. 'The destruction is so awful, & the people so *wonderful* – they *deserve* a better world.' And after the bombing of Buckingham Palace: 'I'm glad we've been bombed. It makes me feel I can look the East End in the face.'

The King's restless mind ceaselessly occupied itself with the search for ways in which he could serve or encourage others. In 1940 he announced the creation of the George Cross and Medal to award to civilians who were excluded from the military medals; and it was his own idea to award the George Cross to Malta when the full weight of Italian and German bombing were used to reduce this vital point in our communications with North Africa. It was he who insisted on paying a surprise visit to the island on his return from visiting the troops in Northern Africa.

'On Sunday at 8.15 a.m.,' he wrote, 'I was on the bridge as we came in to the Grand Harbour. Every bastion & every view point [were] lined with people who cheered as we entered. It was a very moving moment for me. I had made up my mind that I would take a risk to get to Malta & I had got there & by sea. Mussolini called the Mediterranean Sea his Italian Lake a short time ago.'

It would be wrong, too, to think that the King's power to please and encourage was confined to the great mass of the population. President Roosevelt and Winston

Churchill, as well as innumerable others, both attached very special importance to their friendship and contacts with him. The King wrote many formal letters to Roosevelt and took every opportunity to press the hopes and claims of his Government himself, but his personal correspondence with the President was possibly even more important. When Harry Hopkins, the President's special adviser and personal assistant was in England in 1941 he told the King he should write 'more informal letters to F.D.R. as he likes to receive [these] communications'. And in 1942 when Mrs Roosevelt stayed at Buckingham Palace, the President wrote:

> 'I want you and the Queen to tell Eleanor everything in regard to problems of our troops in England which she might not get from Government or military authorities. You and I know that it is the little things which count but which are not always set forth in official reports.'

Most important of all was the King's relationship with Winston Churchill.

In the early summer of 1940 when Neville Chamberlain was forced to resign and Churchill succeeded him, George VI did not personally rejoice in the choice. Churchill had been almost alone in opposition to the Government at the time of the Abdication and had had a long, uneven political career.

'I cannot yet think of Winston as PM,' the King wrote in his diary on 11 May. 'I met Halifax in the garden. I told him I was sorry not to have him as PM.'

Almost at once, however, the King learned to value the heroic personality of the great war leader and the formal audiences between Sovereign and Prime Minister soon gave way to regular luncheons every Tuesday.

'As a convinced upholder of constitutional monarchy,' Churchill wrote later, 'I valued as a signal honour the gracious intimacy with which I, as first Minister, was treated, for which I suppose there has been no precedent since the days of Queen Anne and Marlborough during his years of power.'

On 5 November 1942 after the Eighth Army defeated the German and Italian forces under Rommel's command the King wrote a long letter to Winston Churchill in his own hand to congratulate him. After saying that he knew that the elimination of the Afrika Corps was the most important of all the many operations with which the Prime Minister had to deal he went on:

> 'When I look back & think of all the many arduous hours of work you have put in, & the many miles you have travelled, to bring this battle to such a successful conclusion you have every right to rejoice; while the rest of our people will one day be very thankful to you for what you have done. I cannot say more.'

Here is an account written by Harold Nicolson after lunching with the Churchills in a basement of No. 10 Downing Street on the following day, 6 November.

> 'In a few minutes Winston comes in. He is dressed in his romper suit of Air Force blue and carries a letter in his hand.... He gives the letter to Clemmie. It is a

long letter from the King written in his own handwriting, and saying how much he and the Queen have been thinking of Winston these glorious days. Winston is evidently pleased. "Every word", he mutters, "in his own hand." '

The King followed the course of the war on all fronts very closely and the entries in his diary show how well-informed he was on every issue. He longed, as his brother had before him, for a more active role in the political sphere or with his forces on the battle front. Once war was declared and his Ministers were no longer so much disturbed by questions of prestige and loss of face, they often turned to him to appeal directly to the rulers of Europe – King Leopold of the Belgians, Petain, King Boris of Bulgaria, King George of Greece, Prince Paul of Yugoslavia. He may have had some influence with Prince Paul, with whom like other members of the Royal Family he was on terms of close personal friendship, but the most he could do was to defer the day when the Prince felt it necessary to succumb to German pressure. The King's appeals were thwarted, as was so much else, by the long failure of the British to re-arm. No effective appeal could be made to the countries of Europe while it could not be backed by military might or the weapons of war, without which they were unable to withstand the might of the German armies.

But the King was patient and modest and without any of the *folie de grandeur* which had caused his brother publicly to criticise his Ministers and privately to go behind their backs in talks with representatives of foreign, even hostile, powers. In the long run he accepted with gratitude as well as resignation his unique power to encourage and console and he travelled thousands of miles to visit the troops. 'A visit from me would buck them up,' he would say, and, although his health was never good and in Northern Africa he suffered much from 'Desert tummy', he never saved himself. 'It was certainly worth doing', he wrote to his mother with his habitual understatement, 'and did me a great deal of good. I feel I have done some good to the troops who have fought so well.' And in spite of recording in his diary that 'I hate broadcasting', he carried on his father's tradition of broadcasting to the nation at Christmas and at other appropriate times.

In private life he and his family lived with a complete simplicity which matched the severity of the restrictions imposed upon their subjects. When Mrs Roosevelt stayed at Buckingham Palace she was struck chiefly by the cold. 'Buckingham Palace is an enormous place, and without heat,' she wrote. 'I do not see how they keep the dampness out.' She was also surprised by the food which, although served on gold or silver plate was the same, Lord Woolton informed her, as 'might have been found in any home in England and which would have shocked the King's grandfather'.

When the King and Queen went to Sandringham on the rare occasions when they could rest, they stayed at Appleton, a Victorian house hardly bigger than many of the rectories of England, which had been bought orginally for Edward VII's daughter, Queen Maud of Norway.

It was true that the King had inherited many of the qualities of his father. He was an absolute stickler for clothes. It was not merely that he interested himself in all questions touching uniforms or medals, he was perfectly capable of putting people right about the details of their civilian clothes. The look of amusement and expostulation on his face in the photograph on p. 71 is caused by the vision in a line of men he was reviewing of Mr Fellowes (later Sir William), in private life the agent at Sandringham, dressed in a regulation battle dress. He also had very strong views on matters concerning his family as well as great familiarity with matters of rank, both characteristic of his predecessors. On Princess Elizabeth's eighteenth birthday there was an agitation for her to be made Princess of Wales. 'I argued that it was a family matter ' he wrote. And in a letter to Queen Mary: 'How could I create Lilibet the Princess of Wales when it is the recognised title of the wife of the Prince of Wales. Her own name is so nice and what name would she be called by when she marries, I want to know.'

He had an unyielding loyalty to his friends. The year 1945, in which he shared to the full the national rejoicing, was marred for him, not merely by the death of President Roosevelt, but by the loss of power of the Conservative Party under Winston Churchill at the General Election. The King mourned the loss of President Roosevelt and of Winston Churchill he wrote in his diary:

'I saw Winston at 7.0 pm & it was a very sad meeting. I told him I thought the people were very ungrateful after the way they had been led in the War . . . I asked him if I should send for Mr Attlee to form a Government and he agreed. We said good-bye & I thanked him for all his help to me during the 5 War Years.'

The King and Queen
at Balmoral.

Queen Elizabeth.

King George VI.

The Queen with Princess Elizabeth and Princess Margaret.

The King and Queen pictured soon after the war.

SIX

KING AND QUEEN: IN PEACE

I T FELL TO King George VI to rule during the period of the first Labour Government with a working majority in the House of Commons, and to preside over the first steps in the shedding of Great Britain's colonial power.

The Labour Government of 1945 aroused political passions unknown in England since 1911. In retrospect it is regarded as, in its early days, a good reforming government. Many of the measures implemented by it had been accepted by the wartime coalition government, and it is hard to understand now the bitterness which was engendered by the introduction of the National Health Service. Anger was aroused, not only because these measures were accompanied by the nationalisation of the coal mines, railways, road transport, gas and electricity as well as the Bank of England 'which, to the surprise of many, was revealed to be already in an advanced stage of nationalization', but because the tensions, inevitably caused by the transfer of power from the old ruling class to the new, were the source of emotions of an undisguisedly primitive kind. Hot heads in the Labour Party, notably Aneurin Bevan, were unnecessarily offensive (as Lloyd George had been before them), while members of the upper classes, although anxious to defend themselves against the charge of obstructing progress, were too much disturbed by the sudden and, as it happened, totally unexpected loss of power to view impartially the performance of the Labour Party.

It was a great shock to the King to lose Churchill and he was bound to feel apprehensive at the prospect of a new and untried Government in the circumstances of the day. In addition, he stood at the centre and apex of the very society whose structure was so clearly threatened and whose emotional disturbance he naturally shared. The Royal Family, from Queen Victoria onwards, had shown themselves far more genuinely concerned about the lot of the poor and far more humane in their outlook than the majority of the aristocracy and industrialists, but it is ludicrous to pretend that the King could have embraced any political philosophy other than that of the old ruling classes. 'He himself', his biographer writes, 'was a progressive in political thought and a reformer in social conscience but he was distrustful of undue haste and of political extremism in any form.' This, of course, was the Conservative position, and it was exactly the disillusion with gradualism, the belief that no time could ever be the right time for measures they felt absolutely necessary, which had caused such a large defection to the Labour Party of those who held the middle ground.

Moreover, the King's views were bound to be much affected by the opinions of the people he would ordinarily meet. 'I was doing my best to warn them that they were going too fast in their legislation,' he said to a friend, 'and were offending every class of people who were ready to help them if they were asked to, but were swept aside by regulations etc.' In the latter part of this speech there lies a deep misconception of the possibility of compromise between those now in opposition and the Labour Party.

> 'It was clear that there could be no return to past conditions [Atlee wrote]. The old pattern was worn out and it was for us to weave the new ... We had not been elected to try to patch up an old system but to make something new. Our policy was not a reformed capitalism, but progress towards a democratic socialism.'

The King behaved with absolute integrity, courtesy and consideration and he showed a strong desire to get on terms with his new Ministers. But it worried him. Neither he nor his government yet understood that for many years the welfare of Great Britain would depend more on world events than on anything she could do for herself. If he had known that his country stood at the beginning of years of economic difficulty and loss of power, he might have felt less personal responsibility. As it was, it was a strain to deal with new Ministers, in whose policies he had, at any rate at first, no great confidence. 'I have asked Mr Attlee 3 times now if he is not worried over the domestic situation in this country,' he wrote in January 1947, 'But he won't tell me he is when I feel he is. I know I am worried.' And later he wrote to Queen Mary: 'I do wish one could see a glimmer of a bright spot anywhere in world affairs. Never in the whole history of mankind have things looked gloomier than they do now, and one feels so powerless to do anything to help.'

The King's life was not made easier during the period of the Labour Government by the personality of Mr Attlee, who probably had less of the social arts than any Prime Minister in British history, and who was incapable of a show of grace even to his most humble supporter much less to the King. At the beginning of their association the audiences the King gave his Prime Minister were therefore notable chiefly for the long silences between them. In the end both learned to understand the other (they had more in common than might have been suspected) and they ended on good terms.

Yet the trouble probably lay deeper than the art of communication. The King has the right to be consulted by his Ministers and the duty 'to encourage and to warn', an unenviable task given the complexities of that time, and one which must, as in all relationships, depend to a large extent on the coincidence of interests and opinions between the giver of advice and the recipients. During the period of the

1945 Government the King was forced to adapt not merely to the new faces but to the conditions of the day. His biographer tells us: 'He was aware that in his talks with Ministers, he was not infrequently successful in presenting arguments which caused them to reconsider decisions at which they had already arrived.' But Keith Middlemas has argued as follows:

'Terms appropriate to the modern exchanges between King and ministers were evolved in these years, answering to a great extent the questions raised before the war about the sovereign's implicit links with one sector of society rather than another. They involved greater formality and a greater distance between them, as individuals, and reflected, naturally, the true political balance. The real friendliness of his first three Prime Ministers, Baldwin, Chamberlain and Churchill, may have disguised the limits of the Crown's influence, just as the extent to which the King absorbed their ideas and followed their policies encouraged him to think that they listened, perhaps more than they did.'

The evidence is not available on which to judge between these conflicting opinions. Nevertheless, given the socialist philosophy but also the fact that the Labour Ministers were by no means immune to the charm and authority of the Royal Family, it seems likely that sometimes one was correct, sometimes the other.

His new Ministers were constantly surprised by the extent of the King's knowledge and his extraordinary attention to detail and, aware of this, he enjoyed asking unexpectedly penetrating questions. In one of the earliest demonstrations of his understanding of the political situations, he disagreed with Attlee over his intention to appoint Hugh Dalton Foreign Secretary and was almost certainly influential in the subsequent appointment of Ernest Bevin. He got on very well with Bevin, just as his father had with J. H. Thomas, and he was not impervious to the charm of the far more extreme Aneurin Bevan. 'I asked him how he liked the responsibility of a Government Dept. instead of criticising it,' the King wrote. 'He laughed at that. I found him easy to talk to.'

From 15 August 1947 the King ceased to sign himself George R I and signed George R. The transfer of power to the Dominions of India and Pakistan, when it finally took place, was one of the most remarkable acts in British history and not least because the Viceroy who conducted the last negotiations was a cousin of the King. Lord Mountbatten, a brilliantly able and successful war leader, at that time at the height of his powers, possessed of consummate nerve as well as imagination and charm, was chosen by Attlee, as 'the one man who might pull it off'. The King, who had previously been unconvinced of the wisdom of any precipitate transfer of power and deeply worried about the future of the Muslims – 'I have always said that India has got to be *governed* and that will have to be our policy,' he had written to Churchill – but who had become reconciled to the necessity to withdraw with as little bloodshed as possible, was additionally reassured by this choice. Lord Mountbatten made it plain that he 'welcomed the fact that his task was to end one régime and inaugurate another'.

Both India and Pakistan wished to remain in the Commonwealth but, since India was to become a republic, it took many months to find a formula under which she could do so. In the end it was agreed that the King should not be the Head of India but of the Commonwealth and in that capacity the Indians would owe him allegiance. The new title, which also took account of the fact that Eire had seceded from the Commonwealth, was used formally for the first time at the coronation of his daughter, who was proclaimed as:

> 'Queen Elizabeth the Second, by the Grace of God Queen of this Realm and of all her other Realms and Territories, Head of the Commonwealth, Defender of the Faith.'

The King would never be free from anxiety and disappointment, however, and the last years of his life saw the Korean war and an adverse turn in world trade. 'It is curious', he wrote to Queen Mary in 1950, 'how Balmoral is always the place where one worries most, but on the whole it is worth it, as one can get out & away from it all for a few hours. I held a Privy Council here to sign the Proclamation for the Bank Holiday, but it was so secret that I could not tell anybody about the £ devaluation. I fear it is only a palliative & not a cure for our financial position.'

Yet he must be counted a happy man. On Princess Elizabeth's wedding day, her father wrote to her as follows:

> 'I was so proud of you & thrilled at having you so close to me on our long walk in Westminster Abbey, but when I handed your hand to the Archbishop I felt that I had lost something very precious. You were so calm & composed during the Service & said your words with such conviction, that I knew everything was all right.
>
> 'I am so glad you wrote and told Mummy that you think the long wait before your engagement & the long time before the wedding was for the best. I was rather afraid that you had thought I was being hard hearted about it. I was so anxious for you to come to South Africa as you knew. Our family, us four, the "Royal Family" must remain together with additions of course at suitable moments!! I have watched you grow up all these years with pride under the skilful direction of Mummy, who as you know is the most marvellous person in the World in my eyes, & I can, I know, always count on you, & now Philip, to help us in our work. Your leaving us has left a great blank in our lives but do remember that your old home is still yours & do come back to it as much & as often as possible. I can see that you are sublimely happy with Philip which is right but don't forget us is the wish of
>
> Your ever loving & devoted Papa.'

No daughter in all the land can ever have received a more touching letter, and, if we had no other evidence of the King's nature, we should still understand why he was so much loved by his wife and daughters. He had grown to his position, and it is doubtful whether, after some years had passed, he would have exchanged his role for any other, in spite of all the toil and disappointments. Yet he remained a private person and his happiness was because he was both loved and loving.

He had, too, other sources of contentment. The Royal Family are seen by the public only on ceremonial occasions and it is sometimes insufficiently understood that they are by nature primarily country people. Their fondness for their horses and dogs is only less than for their nearest and dearest friends, and in their leisure hours at Sandringham and Balmoral they walk and ride and shoot and fish, living hard and taking more air and exercise than many of their countrymen ever do.

The King and Queen loved gardening and in all their many homes they supervised the garden, although the one at Royal Lodge remains most especially their own. The King was, of the two, the landscape gardener, giving much thought to the effect of opening up drives and clearing woodlands and showing, it is said, a natural sense of proportion, while the Queen loved flowers and scent.

But the King's great passion in life was shooting. There is an account by Aubrey Buxton of George VI as sportsman which tells us indirectly so much about his character that it is a source no biographer should ignore. The King was a good shot and this, like the ability to play games, is due to physical attributes not everyone possesses. It requires co-ordination of eye and limb, an alert and spontaneous reaction and, as in games, speedy footwork. The King had all these things in good measure and he might have been a first-class shot had he had the right temperament. But as a keeper put it on being asked if the King was a fast shot, 'Too fast'. He added that he often thought the King had missed his first bird in his anxiety to make sure of his second. There is no doubt, however, of his physical prowess. In the winter of 1947 the ponds at Sandringham froze over and everyone played ice hockey. Of all the company the King had only one equal in skill. And shooting to him was much more than an expression of skill, because he developed into a sportsman and naturalist. In his youth at Sandringham he had been trained to the big shoots when everything was artificially prepared to ensure sport – birds reared in quantity, the woodlands laid out to ensure a low flight, dozens of beaters to bring them on to the line of shots and success measured in terms of the carcases at the end of the day. But at Glamis the King was introduced by his brothers-in-law to the joys of rough shooting, a sport which requires unlimited patience, indifference to the weather, understanding of the habits of game, and which is not primarily concerned with the size of the bag but which yields an infinite variety of experience.

'The charm of solitude, the fascination of the marshland and awakening, the changing pattern of the sky, the other birds seen you do not shoot – all these things lure the sportsman who is a countryman or naturalist as well ... Such a man must surely derive more from the ordinary day driving or walking up game. Between spasms of shooting the day is packed with interest. The sky is seldom empty, a woodland never lifeless. Because of his understanding and knowledge this man is always alert, anticipating, looking in the most likely places to watch some small interlude of the wild. To be in the country is his first objective, to bag the game by ingenuity and understanding the next.'

Later King George became an enthusiastic wild fowler, a sport which is even more unpredictable, since it depends on the movement of migratory duck.

Yet, if the times when he walked all day with a few companions, sometimes even alone, were to him the best of all, the accounts of the more formal days also tell us a great deal about him. He never lost his kindness and sensitivity to the feelings of others. He was regarded as always modest in the numbers of birds he claimed but, should some young man who was not very experienced be beside him his claims would be even lower than usual. He never could bear the discomfiture of others.

As he grew older he grew more like his father. He was a great stickler – for punctuality, for clothes, for manners. It is a characteristic of the Royal Family to attach a quite extraordinary importance to clothes. King Edward VII had a whole evening ruined because Lord Rosebery wore the wrong tie, while King George V spoiled any chance of an understanding with his eldest son (who himself was a stickler of a different kind) by his constant criticism of his taste in clothes. King George VI was at least as knowledgeable as his predecessors and no less particular. An event revealing his meticulous eye and detailed knowledge occurred in connection with Lord Gowrie, VC, who was seen to be wearing among his numerous ribbons the China Medal for the Relief of Peking and Queen Victoria's Medal for the first part of the South African War. Pointing this out to Sir Owen Morshead, the King asked whether he had ever seen the two in conjunction before. 'How on earth did he get from China to South Africa in time?' he asked. The same precision was turned on to the failures or mistakes of his shooting parties and, believing that correct attire was as important to others as to himself, he was not above sending for someone to confide in them that the seam of their stockings was crooked.

He had a very British humour, thinking that jokes, like wine, improve with maturity. Certain places, certain people, certain things would unfailingly produce the same reaction, with no loss of amusement to the King. And indeed old jokes are not uncommon in a closed and affectionate society.

Like most other males of the Royal Family, King George VI was a Freemason. He was initiated in 1919 while in the Navy and in 1924 he became Grand Master of the Masonic Province of Middlesex. What pleased him most was to be received into the Lodge Glamis 99 by the village postman and he was later installed Grand

The King and Queen and Princess Elizabeth on their
Southern Africa tour in 1947.

Above Enjoying the Christmas Concert in a Norfolk village hall in 1947.

Opposite above At Royal Lodge in 1946.

Opposite below The Queen presents the Championship Cup to the proud winner at the Norfolk Show in 1950.

Below In the Royal Box at the Palladium during the Royal Command Performance of 1950.

The King and Queen leaving St George's Chapel, Windsor after the Service of the Knights of the Garter in 1950.

Opposite The King and Queen in the blue drawing-room of Buckingham Palace on their Silver Wedding Anniversary in 1948.

Prince Charles and Princess Anne with their grandparents in 1951.

Master of the Grand Lodge of Scotland. When he became King he had to relinquish these offices but he still retained his belief in the values of the Order. Indeed the depth of his feeling for it is made plain by an entry in his diary which describes his farewell to his brother, the ex-King Edward VIII, on the night when the latter left England as Duke of Windsor. 'When D and I said goodbye', he wrote, 'we kissed, parted as freemasons & he bowed to me as his King.'

The King was ill for several years before he died. His illness began in the autumn of 1948 with cramp and pain in his leg and left foot, which was diagnosed as arteriosclerosis in its early stages. His doctors were sufficiently concerned to insist on the cancellation of his proposed visit to Australia and New Zealand and advised a period of treatment and rest. His health improved considerably as a result of the treatment and his disappointment was therefore all the greater when in the following spring his doctors recommended that he undergo a right lumbar sympathectomy operation. 'So all our treatment has been a waste of time,' he said.

The operation was performed on 12 March 1949 at Buckingham Palace where thousands collected and where the placards of news vendors simply carried the news 'He's all right', when the success of the operation was reported. The King appeared to recover and plans for a tour of Australia and New Zealand were resumed, although even with rest and relaxation he now became very tired. 'Nor', his biographer writes, 'could he, by virtue of his temperament, divorce his mind from anxiety over the affairs of state. "The incessant worries & crises through which we live got me down properly", he wrote to a friend.'

In the spring of 1951 the King developed what was believed to be influenza, but which after exhaustive examination was discovered to be a small area of catarrhal inflammation in the left lung. This appeared to respond to treatment with penicillin and he recovered sufficiently to enjoy a day's shooting but in September he again developed a chill and sore throat. A bronchoscopy for the purpose of removing a portion of tissue from the lung for examination was then carried out and revealed a malignant growth. An operation was performed on the morning of Sunday 23 September and the whole of his left lung was removed.

Once again the King's recovery was satisfactory and by mid-October he wrote to Queen Mary that he was getting stronger and could walk to the bathroom. By Christmas he seemed gay and even carefree and with the approval of his doctors he began shooting soon after he arrived at Sandringham. On the morning of 31 January he stood at London airport to wave good-bye to Princess Elizabeth and the Duke of Edinburgh who left on the first stage of a journey which was intended to be to East Africa, Australia and New Zealand.

5 February was Keepers' Day at Sandringham, traditionally a day of rough sport and on this occasion of perfect weather. The King enjoyed it very much and shot

well. That night he went to bed early and went to sleep, a sleep from which he would not awake.

When the news of the King's death was broadcast, all over Britain people wept, among them many who had never even seen him. His unsparing devotion to them was returned a hundredfold.

SEVEN

THE QUEEN MOTHER

IF ONE WERE TO find oneself on a hill with the mist coming down, or with a punctured tyre on a fifty mile stretch between two French villages, or merely with two hours delay at an airport, it would be a singular stroke of luck if, by some sequence of events it is not easy to imagine, one's companion in distress happened to be Queen Elizabeth, the Queen Mother. For she has an enviable fortitude. The British public know and love Queen Elizabeth for her sympathy, her charm, her interest in them and her delectable appearance. The qualities which have made it possible for her to devote herself for so many years to the public service, which will earn her a place among the few great Royal Consorts and ensure her the endless attention of biographers, are her strength and her extraordinary sense of dedication.

She has been a major influence during the course of two reigns, yet she is not dominating or assertive and, according to those who know her well, she seldom insists, almost invariably suggests. It is the measure of her self-reliance that there is so little outward show. A characteristic story is told of her on an occasion when fire broke out on the *Renown* on which, as Duchess of York, she was returning from Australia. 'Did you ever realise Ma'am,' the Captain asked her after it was over, 'that at the time it was pretty bad.' 'Yes, I did,' she replied. 'Every hour someone came and told me it was nothing to worry about, so I knew there was real trouble.'

Another event connected with Royal tours illustrates an extraordinary devotion to duty. In 1939, when the King and Queen were on their way to Canada, the *Empress of Australia*, on which they sailed, became marooned in dense fog and surrounded by icebergs. Many years later one of the Queen's ladies-in-waiting talked to her about this experience. 'Wasn't it terrible?' she asked. 'Well, yes it was,' Her Majesty answered. 'You see we lost two days of the tour.'

During the King's illness and after his death, it seemed to members of her Household and the King's doctors that her very self-sufficiency put the Queen at risk. All through his illness she thought only of him, sought consolation from no one, and never broke down. After his death she withdrew for many weeks and communed only with herself. No sorrow is more desolating than the sorrow of a widow of a man who loved her, and for a member of the Royal Family the loneliness is doubled. In the letter the King wrote to his daughter on her wedding day, he said: 'Our family, us four, the "Royal Family" must remain together, with additions of course at suitable moments.' There may be several shades of meaning to his careful definitions of 'our family' but one of them must surely be that the only real relationships 'this family, these four' had – in the sense of one between equals – was with each other. The closeness of their ties, their happiness together, has been remarked throughout their lives, and no one can see the late King's wife and daughters together, as happens occasionally, for instance in church, without sensing the strength of the family bond. The King provided not merely his full share of affection but his full share of the fun. Once after a long and tiring function in Buckingham Palace, someone opened a door on to a corridor and caught sight of the King and Queen, hand in hand, skipping gaily down it together. But only when entirely alone could they indulge the spontaneous emotions of relief or happiness which come naturally to all of us.

Today the Royal Family receive more love and admiration than ever before, from those who serve them as well as from the populace, but they live in a state of isolation from the world around them hard for the rest of us to imagine. Queen Elizabeth had never needed anyone but the King. Because of her personality and his difficulties as a young man, his dependence on her has been so much stressed, but she was equally dependent on him. He had been the recipient of all that most wives communicate to their husbands and also all that most of us communicate to our friends. Now that he was gone she needed time. Those closest to her feared for her because she was so unapproachable, but she sought strength, as at all times and as with smaller things, from within herself.

Looking back one can see that no one need seriously have feared she would not find it. At the time of her husband's death she wrote a message to the people all over the world who had sent her messages of love and sympathy. Speaking of her late husband as 'a great and noble King' she went on to say:

'No man had a deeper sense of duty and of service, and no man was more full of compassion for his fellowmen. He loved you all, every one of you most truly. That, you know, was what he always tried to tell you in his yearly message at Christmas; that was the pledge he took at the sacred moment of his Coronation fifteen years ago. Now I am left alone to do what I can to honour that pledge without him.

'Throughout our married life we have tried, the King and I, to fulfil with all our hearts and all our strength the great service that was laid upon us. My only wish now is that I may be allowed to continue the work that we sought to do together.'

No one who gave these words their full meaning, a difficulty with public proclamations, could doubt that, after a breathing space, the Queen would return to the work to which she, too, had pledged herself at the Coronation.

She chose to be known as Queen Elizabeth, the Queen Mother, but because her daughter was named after her, she is known to the public as the Queen Mother,

The Royal Family at Buckingham Palace with Lieutenant Philip Mountbatten,
Princess Elizabeth's fiancé, in 1947.

The King and Queen pictured during their tour of Southern Africa in 1947.

The Queen Mother visits the London School of Fashion in 1965.

At the Badminton Horse Trials in 1976: from left to right Lady Sarah Armstrong Jones, Princess Margaret, Queen Elizabeth the Queen Mother, the Duke of Beaufort and the Queen.

The Queen Mother arrives at Covent Garden for a gala performance.

unlike Queen Mary who was known by that name until the end of her life. For twenty-five years she has undertaken a programme of duties which would daunt the youngest and strongest of us. Her activities are too well known to the British public to need enumeration here but it may not be so generally realised that she has journeyed all over the world, travelling thousands of miles in most years and visiting not merely the countries of the Commonwealth but the United States of America and France again and again.

Her energy is formidable and always a surprise to everyone who accompanies her for the first time. Her unpunctuality is still regarded as her only fault, but that is largely because she will not leave the person she is with or the thing she is doing in the interests of the next one. She is an exacting person to serve. Often she continues to talk to people long after the call of duty has been satisfied and in truth long after those who accompany her are exhausted. One of her ladies-in-waiting once said to her that she felt herself too old for such a demanding job. 'What about me?' Queen Elizabeth replied, and that was the end of that.

'If one has to do something', she once remarked, 'one may as well learn to like it.' But it is doubtful whether she really had to learn. A foreigner at the time of her Coronation remarked that, although she must have laid many a foundation stone, she continued to do it 'as though she had discovered a new and delightful way of spending an afternoon'. Over the years she has acquired an entirely professional technique for expressing what she feels but this does not diminish the strength with which she feels it. It is unavoidable when thinking of her to compare her with others who dedicate themselves to the service of large numbers of people – doctors, priests, nurses. She has that single-minded attention to the person she is with, which blocks out the rest of the world and marks the true vocation.

Queen Elizabeth is very persuasive. 'Before I knew where I was', the organiser of a charity said to one of her ladies-in-waiting, 'I was telling her all my troubles.' 'Everyone always does,' was the reply.

She has considerable public gifts, the most noticeable of which is her ability when moving in a crowd to make individuals feel that she is addressing her attention to each of them. This is felt not merely by old ladies in hospital who are surprised and gratified to find themselves picked out and to people in large crowds all over the world but by all the more sophisticated as well. Harold Nicolson returns to the subject again and again.

'The Queen was superb,' he wrote in 1939. 'She really does manage to convey to each individual in the crowd that he or she have had a personal greeting.' On this occasion he thinks it is because of the brilliance of her eyes. And he adds: 'But she is in truth one of the most amazing Queens since Cleopatra.'

In 1945: 'The Queen has a truly miraculous faculty of making each individual feel that it is him whom she has greeted and to him that was devoted that lovely smile. She has a true genius for her job.'

And in 1958 when he met her at Morley College: 'She was in her best mood and spirits. She has that astonishing gift of being sincerely interested in dull people and dull occasions. Really, the woodwork, the pottery and the drawings with which these Morley students occupy themselves in the evening are horrible objects. But the Queen Mother seemed really interested and spoke to almost all of them.'

While to Chips Channon, the erstwhile friend of Mrs Simpson, who thought George VI 'good, dull, dutiful and good-natured', we owe: 'The Queen saw me and smiled, with a touch of the twinkle she keeps for her old friends.'

The Queen has also highly developed the gift of talking to people. She can walk down a line of men drawn up to meet her and address some personal conversation to each. On a race course she never passes a policeman on horseback without some smiling salutation, usually surprising him not merely by the friendly greeting but by the knowledgeable comment she makes on his horse.

Like most of the Royal Family, the Queen Mother is naturally a countrywoman. She returned to Birkhall from Balmoral when she moved from Buckingham Palace to Clarence House and she kept, of course, her first love, Royal Lodge. Soon after the King's death, while staying with friends in Caithness on the north coast of Scotland, she saw the Castle of Mey which it was feared might be demolished. To save it, she bought it, repaired it and refurnished it. Ever since at certain times of the year, someone walking on the shore just north of John O'Groats might see seals jumping out of the sea in response to the tune of 'See the bonny boats' sung by a small figure in the old blue mackintosh, wearing a blue felt hat into the band of which a red feather had been stuck. If this mythical passerby were to stop and pass the time of day, the friendliness with which his greeting was returned might make him doubt that he was right in recognising Queen Elizabeth, the Queen Mother.

Queen Elizabeth is a particularly warm patron of the arts. She is always ready to lend her presence to a Gala or Benevolent performance of music, or ballet, or of the drama. Quite apart from this she often goes privately with friends to performances at Covent Garden and the Coliseum. She likes things to be well done, and, when Lord Drogheda decided to raise a fund privately to add the third row of lights to the auditorium at Covent Garden (unaccountably left out in the original building), Her Majesty was one of the first people to subscribe to it. Her example made the rest of his task quite easy.

She also loves pictures and, when she can find time, pays a visit to one of the galleries. She has a collection of modern paintings which includes pictures by Sisley, Lowry, Matthew Smith and Augustus John.

But in spite of everything she has always remained a countrywoman. She has to have air and no weather is too bad for her and her dogs to take exercise. She loves to have meals out of doors and she picnics whenever it is possible. In the summer it might surprise motorists in the Mall to know that behind the great plane trees in the garden of St James's Palace, a long table is laid with the luncheon for Queen

Her Majesty Queen Elizabeth, the Queen Mother.

Opposite The Queen Mother taking shelter from a
shower in the house of Mrs H. Jamieson of Herne
Hill, London, during a visit to private gardens.

Right Queen Elizabeth talking to Noël Coward in the
drawing-room at Fairlawne during one of her annual
weekend visits.

Left Devon Loch collapses during the 1956 Grand National. (1) He is running home to win but (2) (3) he makes a sudden leap as he passes the water-jump, then his hindlegs crumple beneath him (4) (5) (6); his forelegs remain rigid (7). The jockey, Dick Francis, is almost unseated by the collapse (8) and is then thrown forward and has to cling on as Devon Loch lurches up again (9) (10). E.S.B. approaches (11) and Devon Loch is up again but stationary and E.S.B. passes to win (12).

Above right Queen Elizabeth and her daughter, the Queen, enter the enclosure to see Devon Loch unsaddled after winning the New Century Chase at Hurst Park in 1955.

Below right Queen Elizabeth presents Peter Cazalet with a whip which once belonged to George II to commemorate her one-hundredth winner. His wife Zara and Sir Martin Gilliat, the Queen Mother's private secretary, are looking on.

Opposite Queen Elizabeth with some of her string of horses in the park at Fairlawne.

Above Queen Elizabeth visiting Gun Dog Trials being held on the Balmoral Estate.

Left The Castle of Mey, Caithness.

Opposite Salmon fishing at Balmoral. Queen Elizabeth with her chief gillie, Mr James Peart, in 1968.

Queen Elizabeth at Royal Lodge in 1970.

Elizabeth's guests; while in Scotland every member of her Household and all her guests are provided with a folding table and chair and find themselves picnicking in all weathers. On one occasion when torrential rain prevented the royal party leaving Birkhall they picnicked in the porch; on another, when someone came unexpectedly in the morning to the Castle of Mey, delaying the Queen's departure, her party went down the garden and through a door and, picking their way through cow pats, ate their luncheon in the nearest field. She is inclined to sayings and attitudes which will be recognised instantly by anyone old enough to have had a Nanny. 'Ah!' she will say, standing in a gale force wind, 'this will blow the germs away.' She never admits to illness herself until she is dropping on her feet, and when others are ill she can barely conceal her belief that they would feel much better if only they would get up and get on with it.

Queen Elizabeth is intrepidly, irrepressibly square, believing that morals and values are absolute, not subject to fashion, and seeing no need to compromise with the views of succeeding generations. She imposes her own standards of behaviour on those she meets and it would be idle to attempt to decide to what extent her authority is attributable to her position. What is certain is that people who take high standards of behaviour for granted do very often succeed in getting them accepted. No one meeting Queen Elizabeth would attempt to entertain her with the kind of faintly malicious talk about her friends which is the small change of much conversation. She loves the British people whether they deserve it or not. 'I think they are wonderful people,' she says with a flash in her eye it would take a brave man to contradict. And it is true that she loves people, not merely as you and I do, charming or entertaining people, but all the suffering people she meets.

She has a talent for mimicry. Natural mimics do not merely speak with other people's voices, in some way they parody their thoughts and the words they habitually choose. No mimic, however high-minded, can conceal a slightly satirical streak. Queen Elizabeth also has tremendous powers of enjoyment.

Among the things she enjoys most is her racing stable. The Queen first acquired a steeple-chaser in 1949 in partnership with her daughter Princess Elizabeth. Peter Cazalet was asked to find them a horse and he bought an Irish-bred steeple-chaser called *Monaveen*, a half-brother to a famous horse called *Cromwell*, which belonged to Anthony Mildmay and was trained in the same stable. 'He was a very sound horse,' Peter Cazalet said, 'tremendously bold and freegoing and he jumped like the wind.' He was the first horse to run for a Queen of England since a horse called *Star* won at Ascot for Queen Anne, and, in Princess Elizabeth's colours, he repeated the victorious performance of his predecessor. He won again at Sandown and he won a big race called *The Queen Elizabeth Steeplechase* at Hurst Park. *Monaveen* thus gave his royal owners tremendous beginners' luck. However, a year later, starting favourite for the same race at Hurst Park, he broke a leg and had to be destroyed.

After Anthony Mildmay's tragic death (from cramp while bathing in the sea) Peter

Cazalet suggested to the Queen that she should buy *Manicou*, one of his very good horses. Princess Elizabeth who was having her first child did not want any further commitment, but her Mother was by now dead keen. 'Who will the Queen share this one with?' Cazalet asked Princess Margaret, and the Princess replied: 'Oh! Mummy wouldn't share with *anybody* now.'

From these beginnings was built up one of the most famous strings of the day. By 1964 Her Majesty reached her 100th winner and by 1970 the score had passed 200. The last winner that Peter Cazalet trained for Queen Elizabeth in March of 1973 – only two months before his death – was *Inch Arran* in the famous Topham Trophy Chase at Liverpool. Peter Cazalet was by then too ill to go to the racecourse, but a film was made of this race and Queen Elizabeth sat beside him at Clarence House while it was shown for him to see. Since his death Her Majesty's horses have been with Fulke Walwyn, and, although she has not so many horses in training now, she has been very successful. At Ascot in February 1976 a horse called *Sunnyboy* scored her 300th win. Every year, as long as Cazalet was alive, she used to stay with him and his wife at Fairlawne for the weekend of the December Lingfield race meeting. On one of her earliest visits Cazalet remarked that she ought to go out in the early morning to see her horses at exercise. Every time she went to Fairlawne after that she was up and out in the park by 7.45. Here is a description of the Royal weekends written by Jim Fairgrieve, Peter Cazalet's Head Lad.

'The Royal Party would come from Lingfield after racing on Friday. Sometimes they would pop into the stables and have a brief look round. Saturday morning, Her Majesty would be on the gallops watching the horses work. It was great to watch her in her wellington boots and headscarf, an icy wind blowing, sometimes a sleety shower. Her head would be up facing the gallops and enjoying every minute of it ... Sunday morning, after church, the Royal Party would go round every horse in the yard, whether they were her Majesty's or not. Every horse had a lump of sugar from the Royal hand and every lad had a word of praise about the look of their charge.'

The Queen Mother came to be regarded as the perfect owner. From the preceding account one can see that she loved the sport for its own sake and loved the animals for theirs. She often had a run of bad luck but this dimmed neither her enthusiasm nor her confidence in those who worked for her. At Liverpool in 1956 she had one of the most spectacular pieces of bad luck in the history of racing. Her horse *Devon Loch* had virtually won the National when something occurred which no one has been able fully to explain. Here is Ivor Herbert's description of it.

'Skirting the elbow bend a furlong from the finish, it would seem he had the race well won being five or six lengths ahead and obviously full of running. Fifty yards from the post Francis the jockey had stopped riding him, when suddenly *Devon*

Loch's hind legs appeared to slip from under him, he staggered and came down with his forefeet under him but did not roll over. Francis retained his seat and the horse struggled to his feet being passed as he did so by *E.S.B.* It still seemed that if only *Devon Loch* could get going again he must yet be second, but though Francis urged him, he was all at sea and seemed temporarily to have lost the use of his legs. Francis now dismounted.'

Several explanations have been put forward about what happened but Ivor Herbert thinks the most likely is that the horse had an attack of cramp. He produces evidence that in the light of this occurrence jockeys who had ridden the horse in the past were inclined to think that something very like it had happened more than once before.

Here is part of a letter from Harold Nicolson to his wife, written a few days later:

'At luncheon yesterday I sat between Michael Adeane and the young Duke of Devonshire. They had been standing with the royal party at Aintree when *Devon Loch* collapsed. They said it was a horrible sight. The public and the people in the enclosure took it for granted that the horse had won and turned towards the royal box and made a demonstration, yelling and waving their hats. Then someone shouted out that there had been an accident, and the ovation stopped suddenly as if a light had been switched off. There was a complete hush. The Princess Royal panted "It can't be true! It can't be true!" The Queen Mother never turned a hair. "I must go down", she said, "and comfort those poor people." So down she went, dried the jockey's tears, patted Peter Cazalet on the shoulder and insisted on seeing the stable-lads who were also in tears. "I hope the Russians saw it," said Devonshire. "It was the most perfect display of dignity that I have ever witnessed." In fact Malenkov and his party were in a box nearby.'

Queen Elizabeth is always prepared to take the rough with the smooth, not merely on the day of the race but also in the preparation for it. In the early fifties she bought some well-bred promising-looking yearlings from Ireland and sent them to Eldred Wilson, a neighbour at Sandringham, to be broken and backed before they went on to Fairlawne to be trained. These youngsters were handpicked by the best judges but they only cost a few hundreds each and any one of them which had been a success in training might have paid for the others. However, although Queen Elizabeth got much enjoyment from watching their progress, with the exception of a horse called *Gay Record* who won nine races, they were all of them failures on the racecourse and the whole idea had quite early to be abandoned. The Queen had more luck, however, with a yearling by her own horse *Manicou* out of a mare belonging to Mr Jack Irwin, the landlord of the *Red Cat* at Wootton Marshes in Norfolk. Hearing that Mr Irwin had a good foal, Queen Elizabeth went to see him. All that year, whenever she was down at Sandringham, she paid a visit to Mr Irwin to have another look at his colt and then when he was a two-year-old, she bought him. This was *The Rip* who ran fifty-one races, winning thirteen of them and being placed sixteen times.

Sandringham is, to the outsider, the least attractive of any of the royal residences. A large Edwardian house, it stands in the middle of flat uninteresting country. Yet it was the most beloved by George V and also by George VI chiefly for the sport it gave them. It is said that it also holds first place in Queen Elizabeth's heart. She visits it whenever she can, and on these occasions the well-informed passerby will often know of her presence because of the sight of her car or of one of her staff near the stables.

In her middle seventies Her Majesty still undertakes a hard day's work, still loves racing, still enjoys a party, still comforts the sad and disappointed. She still impresses foreigners both here and on her travels by her special blend of dignity and informality. Above all she still loves life.

'You must *never* look at your feet, my mother always taught me that,' Queen Elizabeth was instructing a lady-in-waiting how to come downstairs in a long dress with a train. But her words would do as an expression of her philosophy.

ACKNOWLEDGMENTS

Between pages 22 and 31

King George VI aged two   *Mansell Collection*
Queen Elizabeth as a child   *Daily Express*
Lady Elizabeth Bowes-Lyon with her father   *Press Association*
Glamis Castle   *Popperfoto*
Lady Elizabeth Bowes-Lyon aged fourteen   *Mansell Collection*
Group portrait of the royal children   *Mansell Collection*
Queen Mary with Prince Edward and Prince Albert   *Radio Times Hulton Picture Library*
Sandringham   *A. F. Kersting*
Prince Albert   *Mansell Collection*
Lady Elizabeth Bowes-Lyon   *Mansell Collection*
Prince Albert and Lady Elizabeth Bowes-Lyon at the time of their engagement
   Mansell Collection

Between pages 38 and 47

Wedding portrait   *By gracious permission of H.M. the Queen*
Family group portrait on the wedding day   *By gracious permission of H.M. the Queen*
Duke and Duchess of York leaving Buckingham Palace after the reception   *Popperfoto*
Duke and Duchess of York on honeymoon   *Popperfoto*
Duchess of York at a coconut shy   *Radio Times Hulton Picture Library*
Duke of York at Wimbledon   *Radio Times Hulton Picture Library*
Duchess of York fishing in New Zealand   *Popperfoto*
Duke and Duchess of York visit a factory   *Radio Times Hulton Picture Library*
Duke of York watching a Scout Jamboree   *Radio Times Hulton Picture Library*
The Yorks arriving in Skye   *Popperfoto*
King Edward VIII with Mrs Simpson in a nightclub   *Popperfoto*
King Edward VIII on holiday with Mrs Simpson   *Popperfoto*

Between pages 52 and 61

The Coronation   *Radio Times Hulton Picture Library*
The King at the Boys' Boxing Championship   *Popperfoto*

The Queen Mother talking to Noël Coward   (*Private Collection*)
Devon Loch collapses in the Grand National   *Tophams Ltd/Movietone News*
The Queen Mother with the Queen at Hurst Park races   (*Private Collection*)
The Queen Mother presents Peter Cazalet with a whip   (*Private Collection*)
The Queen Mother with some of her string of horses   (*Private Collection*)
The Queen Mother visiting Gun Dog Trails   *Popperfoto*
Castle of Mey   *British Tourist Authority*
Salmon fishing at Balmoral   *Popperfoto*
The Queen Mother at Royal Lodge in 1970   *Cecil Beaton*

Picture research by Caroline Lucas

INDEX

Page numbers in *italic* refer to the illustrations